"From the first few gorgeous (like *beyond* gorgeous) photos to the creative and tantalizingly delicious table of contents, Nichole sold me on *Scandinavian Everyday* the moment I cracked its spine. This book speaks to the snacker in me, as well as the tinned fish lover (who knew I was an oven-smoked salmon lover, too?) and everything in between. And, yes, I might just be celebrating my next birthday with Swedish Sandwich Cake (if you know, you know), alongside some Danish Meringue Puffs, for good measure. What a special book."

—**Jessie Sheehan**, author of *Snackable Bakes*

"In *Scandinavian Everyday*, Nichole Accettola shows us how organic food can connect us to the land and to one another. Her recipes honor farmers, seasonal produce, the skill in the kitchen, and the care it takes to bring these ingredients to the table."

—**Alice Waters**

Scandinavian Everyday

Vibrant, Simple Meals from Northern Europe

Nichole Accettola

Photographs by Molly DeCoudreaux and Mikkel Vang

TEN SPEED PRESS
California | New York

To my children, thank you all for the meals we share.

CONTENTS

LARDER 39

BOWL ME OVER 73

NEW CLASSICS 191

SIMPLE BREADS AND SWEET TREATS 221

LANDING IN SCANDINAVIA

When someone asks me what Scandinavian food is, I always hesitate. Should I start with something familiar, like IKEA's Swedish meatballs, or dive into a story about eating live ants at Noma? Summing up an entire region's food culture in a few sentences feels impossible. It's not just about the recipes; it's the memories, the people, and the settings that give the food its meaning.

For me, Scandinavian cooking is about simplicity and good flavor. I think of a hearty, steaming bowl of savory 3-grain porridge with kale, mushrooms, and farmers cheese (page 81), or crusty toast covered with small, crushed golden potatoes, dollops of crème fraîche, a shower of chives, and bright pearls of fish roe. I also fantasize about devouring salmon-and-corn chowder and licking the bowl clean afterward, just as I can envision being seated at a long table with a group of friends, everyone with sleeves rolled up, cracking open small crayfish shells and saying "Cheers" in the waning late summer light.

These Scandinavian food memories have stayed with me for years. They took my professional cooking career in a new direction; gave me the courage to open Kantine, my Scandinavian-inspired eatery in San Francisco; and inspired me to write my first cookbook, *Scandinavian from Scratch*. That book focused on baking (which I will always adore), but there's so much more to Scandinavian cuisine than pastries and bread. There are also the daily meals—those that nourish us, fuel us, and remind us that even the simplest everyday food can be both doable and meaningful.

This book is written for people who want to cook (and eat) well and simply at home—for those of us who enjoy having a say in what ingredients go into our food and who appreciate meals made from whole, seasonal ingredients. *Scandinavian Every Day* is a collection of my most beloved Scandinavian recipes, those I cooked countless times during my sixteen years living in Denmark and now prepare for my family at home and for my customers at Kantine.

I grew up in the rolling hills outside of Cleveland, Ohio, surrounded by green pastures and cornfields; it was the sort of place where the occasional cow-tipping adventure was not unheard of. In our home, the kitchen was the heart of it all. My mom spent most of her time there, and she made sure we ate at least one meal together as a family every day, usually dinner. (How thinking of that makes me miss her!)

After high school, I followed my heart to the Culinary Institute of America in Hyde Park, New York. It was there that my understanding of food expanded far beyond the meat-starch-vegetable framework I grew up with. On weekends, my friends and I would head to New York City, pooling our limited budgets to eat at as many great restaurants as we could afford. Places like Jean-Georges's JoJo and André Soltner's Lutèce were eye-opening, teaching me that a plate could be more than just food—it could be a story, an art form, or even an escape. It was liberating to let go of the rigid ideas I'd grown up with and immerse myself in everything I could learn. When I wasn't eating out, I became completely engrossed in cookbooks like Marco Pierre White's *White Heat,* the royal-blue *River Café Cookbook, Chez Panisse Menu Cookbook,* and *Bread Alone.*

After graduation, I moved to Boston to attend Boston University's School of Hospitality Administration, where I earned a degree before diving into the city's vibrant restaurant scene. Working in upscale kitchens was thrilling, but over time the relentless pace was mentally and physically exhausting. Eventually, I found myself burned out and longing for something different—some sort of balance. That's when I decided to follow a dream I'd held for years: to live abroad. In 1999, I packed my bags and moved to Copenhagen, Denmark, ready for a new chapter in both life and cooking.

Scandinavian cuisine—the collective foods from Denmark, Norway, and Sweden—has evolved tremendously since I first moved abroad. Back then, meals at home were hearty and solid—meat, potatoes, and brown sauce ruled the day—and they lacked the freshness and vibrancy we now associate with Nordic cooking. The idea of eating locally and seasonally wasn't even a topic of conversation, let alone a movement.

My first trips to Danish grocery stores back then were so very different from what I was accustomed to in the United States. The selection of produce was quite limited and clearly dominated by root vegetables like potatoes, beets, carrots, and celery root. At first, I felt limited by the lack of variety, but ultimately, I saw it as a challenge—an invitation to be more creative amid the constraints. Over time, farmers' markets started popping up, local and organic options became the norm, and even home cooks began embracing plant-forward meals. Suddenly, dishes like Mung Bean Fritters with Goat Cheese (page 139) or a salad of Spice-Roasted Beet, Winter Squash, and Fennel (page 124) didn't seem so unusual—they became part of our everyday repertoire and a path toward a healthy, more sustainable way of eating.

Contemporary Scandinavian food is mouthwateringly delicious; it's made with an abundance of seasonal ingredients, nuts, seeds, good oils and dairy, whole grains, quality meat from neighboring woods or pastures, and sustainable fish from nearby waters. It's food that is brined and smoked, cured and pickled, marinated and sprouted, or often just served raw with a sprinkle of salt. It's approachable, fresh, vibrant food, made with ease in the home kitchen.

ROYAL

A NEW REPERTOIRE

Before moving to Denmark, I had been professionally cooking Italian and French food, and I felt very attached to those traditions, despite never having worked in Italy or France. Living in Denmark and learning to cook Scandinavian foods—especially while Denmark was going through a culinary rejuvenation in the early 2000s—gave me a unique opportunity to experience the cuisine up close. Fueled by curiosity and experimentation, I began to understand what made Scandinavian cuisine distinct. I cooked from classic cookbooks, re-creating dishes that many Scandinavians had almost forgotten, and then I reimagined them in a way that reflected a more modern world. My skills as a chef remained the same, but I was gently nudged toward a way of cooking that felt more intuitive, genuine, and, because I was living in the motherland, deeply personal. It allowed me to dive into my own interpretations of a cuisine, and when I did that, I fell in love with food and cooking all over again. Cooking was no longer about impressing restaurant guests with elaborate dishes; it became about connection: to the seasons, to the people at the table, and to the way in which we are all brought together.

My first encounters with Scandinavian food happened as I settled into my new life in Denmark. I ate my way through each and every holiday, struck up conversations with the local fishmongers, foraged with friends, nurtured my first sourdough starter, and spent countless hours cooking with my small children as they perched beside me on stools. Weekly trips to farmers' markets taught me about Nordic seasons, which because of differences in climate means that some seasons are a lot shorter than those I was familiar with while living on the East Coast of the United States. Often I'd fill my bike basket so full with market produce that steering home became a real challenge. At work, I led cooking classes to inspire others to make food from scratch, and then after hours, conversations with like-minded colleagues sparked alternative ways of thinking about food.

I didn't realize it then, but this new way of living was carving out a space I'd grow into for years to come while living abroad. Stepping away from restaurant life gave me room to exhale, recover, and reengage passionately in culinary whims and projects—steps that ultimately fueled my desire to open Kantine.

Many of the principles of Scandinavian cuisine I learned during my first years abroad have since become part of the foundation of the Nordic diet (see The Nordic Diet, page 24). It's not a diet tied to weight loss or making meals solely with Nordic ingredients, but rather a "food" mindset to follow: Eat locally and seasonally, reduce food waste, and focus on plant-based meals. It calls for a heightened awareness—one that extends to ourselves, our future, and our planet—especially as we navigate a world in desperate need of change. That change starts with us: our habits, our lifestyles, and our plates.

Cooking is more than just preparing meals—it's a reflection of values, of how we choose to nourish ourselves and those around us. For me, learning to cook Scandinavian meant embracing simplicity at a deeper level, where flavor and integrity remain intact. Each recipe in this book is rooted in tradition but has been updated with a contemporary, nourishing twist. The recipes are straightforward and unfussy, letting the goodness of the ingredients shine. They encourage us to be mindful of the seasons, to make the most of what we have, and to find joy in the simple act of gathering. It is a way of cooking that has shaped me, and one that I hope will inspire you to find joy in using food and mealtimes to nourish yourself, your loved ones, and the planet we share.

KITCHEN BEST PRACTICES

My love for food runs deep, and it's a feeling I try to nurture in my family, too. If food is one of life's basic needs, why not make it one of life's greatest pleasures as well?

Here are some of the tried-and-true practices that help make our kitchen the heart of our home.

PLAN FOR FUTURE MEALS BUT STAY FLEXIBLE

In our house, meal planning happens on Sunday afternoons during our weekly family meeting. We look at the week ahead, get an idea of who's doing the cooking and when, and plan accordingly. Not every detail needs to be in place, just enough to know what main ingredients we'll need. While some friends insist on shopping just once a week, I prefer more frequent trips to allow for spontaneity, like a specific craving or when our sons' friends stay for dinner. With a well-stocked fridge and pantry, and by staying adaptable, we're always able to pull together something delicious.

SHARE RESPONSIBILITY

Cooking doesn't have to be a solitary task. In my home, we all take turns in the kitchen, each with our own method and style. I like to get creative with whatever's on hand, whereas my partner prefers to cook under the guidance of recipes. Our two teenagers each cook one dinner of their choosing per week. It's been amazing to watch their skills grow. My oldest son is especially good at breading and frying chicken for homemade chicken nuggets. If things go sideways for them, they know they can call on me to jump in as their sous chef—a role I secretly love. It gives us a chance to connect, be creative together, and share valuable skills.

SHOP SMART

Shopping for food starts before I even leave the house. I always make a complete list and grab a snack before I go so I'm less tempted by impulse buys (though I'll admit, the chip aisle is still my weak spot!). Ideally, I start at the farmers' market for fruits and vegetables, then head to the grocery store for the rest. I try to stick to my list and buy in manageable quantities, so I can keep tabs on what's in the kitchen. The bulk section is especially handy for stocking up on grains and beans without overcommitting.

KEEP IT ORDERLY

We've moved more times than I can count, and as tiring as it can be, I always get a little giddy about unpacking the new kitchen. A well-functioning kitchen comes from mindful choices and good organization. It's not just about what goes where but how the space can be transformed into a practical workplace that supports the way we want to eat.

I store my favorite ingredients as well as my most frequently used tools and cookware front and center. It's both for easy access and visibility—that way, I'm more apt to use these items.

A cluttered kitchen can really detract from the pleasure of cooking, so I remind myself to get rid of equipment I don't use anymore and instead hold on to the chosen few: sharp, well-balanced knives, sturdy cutting boards, and reliable cookware.

CULTIVATE INSPIRATION

Inspiration for cooking can come from anywhere—a trip to the farmers' market, a conversation with a neighbor, or a recipe passed down through family. Sometimes, it's as simple as catching a glimpse of a beautiful ingredient or the taste of something unforgettable while traveling. Dishes born out of curiosity or the urge to re-create often open the door to a deeper understanding of cooking—and spark inspiration to keep you exploring the wondrous world of food.

No matter your level of experience, follow your curiosity. Step beyond your comfort zone to try dishes that intrigue you. Cooking with wonder turns the kitchen into a space for creativity and enjoyment, even if there's some trial and error along the way. Just have faith and keep trying!

BE GREEN

A core principle of the Nordic diet is to cook and eat in a way that is mindful of the environment. At Kantine, we've made sustainable kitchen practices a priority since the beginning, and it's since rubbed off on the way we "run" our kitchen at home.

CONTINUED

ETS FØRSTE
DANSKE ÆRTER
50,-

Here are a few of my favorite kitchen habits:

Label and date leftovers: Masking tape and a permanent marker are always within arm's reach in the kitchen. Clear labeling helps everyone see what's being stored, especially in the fridge, so it can either be eaten or transformed into something new before it spoils.

Save vegetable trimmings: We keep a lidded container in our fridge or freezer—depending on how often we're cooking—to collect scraps like onion peels, carrot, celery, and leek tops, and mushroom and herb stems. Once it's full, we use it to make a flavorful, homemade broth.

Compost: In San Francisco, we're lucky to have curbside composting, but for those without it, there are excellent indoor composting and food recycling systems that help private households be greener. Check with your city or county waste management department for details on programs in your area.

Plan meals around the ingredients in your kitchen: Once you've thinned those out, there's space for a fresh round of new ingredients.

Store vegetables properly so they last longer: A lot of produce keeps well in the refrigerator, but some items, such as garlic, onion, shallots, and potatoes, do best in a cool, dark spot in the kitchen. Remember that fruits like apples and bananas give off a gas that vegetables like cabbage, broccoli, and eggplant can't tolerate, so you'll want to keep these two categories separated in the refrigerator.

Give leftovers a second life: Last night's roasted vegetables can go into today's salad or Vegetable and Bean Hash (page 208). Stale bread makes great croutons or spiced breadcrumbs for a Celery Root, Kale, and Parsley Salad (page 105). With kids, I find that the best way to use leftover vegetables undetected is to puree them and add the puree to a dish like pasta with tomato sauce, chili, or soup.

Get creative with stems and stalks: Broccoli stems (lightly peeled) are great in a crunchy slaw, chard stems can be pickled, and kale stems blend easily into a smoothie.

Dehydrate and grind citrus peels: They add brightness to dressings, baked goods, and teas.

Don't toss wilted greens: Use them in quiches, soups, smoothies, and stews.

Use up dairy before it turns: Yogurt can be whisked into dressings, buttermilk can go into pancakes, and cream can be made into crème fraîche.

Don't let "best by" or "sell by" dates scare you: Use your senses—smell it, taste it, check the texture; you might not want to throw it away. Most foods last longer than the label suggests.

THE NORDIC DIET

Have you ever been on a trip somewhere far away and fallen in love with the foods eaten there or the way that people eat together? I simply adore immersing myself in other places, and frankly, those experiences are some of the best souvenirs I've brought back with me. They enrich my life, put my own way of living in perspective, and sometimes inspire change in our food habits after we've returned home. I'll never forget the look on my kids' faces when I suggested we extend dinnertime to at least an hour for more relaxation and conversation (and the idea of serving a salad course after the main meal was equally unpopular).

Little did I know when I first moved to Denmark that, within a few years, New Nordic cuisine—an approach to cooking that prioritizes local, sustainable, and seasonal ingredients prepared in innovative ways—would emerge, transforming Scandinavia into the culinary hub it is today. This movement not only elevated Nordic cooking globally but also gave rise to the Nordic diet. And while the word "diet" often signals weight loss, this diet is about something else entirely—choosing to eat well with foods rooted in the region's traditions, and shaped with an ecological bent.

While I don't follow the Nordic diet strictly, the general principles are always top of mind for me. If you're familiar with my first cookbook, *Scandinavian from Scratch,* you already know that I'm a firm believer in *fika* (see page 250). Like so many other people, I want to eat well, but that doesn't always mean that my choices are the best for me and/or the planet, so I regularly refer to the parameters of the diet. They remind me of the big picture, and the habits I want to keep.

Rooted in principles similar to the Mediterranean diet, the Nordic diet emphasizes plant-based eating supplemented by other whole foods. The way to eat is broken down into a simple framework:

Eat most often:

Plant-based staples: vegetables, fruits, berries, legumes, and potatoes
Grains and seeds: whole grains like buckwheat, millet, and barley, as well as nuts and seeds
Seafood and dairy: fish, seafood, low-fat dairy products, and eggs
Fats and flavorings: canola oil, herbs, and spices

Eat in moderation:

Cheese, cultured dairy products like yogurt, and game meats

Eat rarely:

Other red meats and animal fats

Avoid or eat very rarely:

Foods with added sugar, processed meats, sugar-sweetened beverages, refined fast foods, and artificial additives

The beauty of the Nordic diet lies in its simplicity and its focus on seasonality. Food that's in season and grown close to where you live isn't just more sustainable—it tastes better. It's easy to embrace seasonality during the summer when market stands are brimming with gorgeous produce, but the same principles apply in the winter as well, despite less seasonal abundance.

Indeed, the diet highlights Nordic food traditions that were derived from century-long practices of harvesting from the earth, the sea, and the forest. Many of those ingredients were preserved to last through the frigidly cold winter months; therefore, techniques such as smoking, curing, and drying have shaped the region's cuisine. Although preservation is much easier today, we still practice these techniques for the delicious flavors they create.

The recipes in this book are inspired by the Nordic approach to food but meant to be adapted in other parts of the world, where lingonberries and lovage are impossible to find. With the principles of the Nordic diet as your guide, you can create nourishing, seasonally driven meals with ingredients that are in sync with your area.

Eating well is vital to staying healthy, but it's just one part of the equation. In Scandinavia, nourishing food combined with a sound work–life balance, social involvement in a community, and a strong connection to nature are key to holistic well-being and fundamental aspects of the Nordic diet.

AUBERGINER
ITALIEN
PR. STK. 20,-
CITRONER
ITALIEN
3 STK. 20,-
DeliFresh
De Benito

THE SCANDINAVIAN PLATE

Scandinavia is part of the Nordic region, so when we refer to the Nordic diet, we are also talking about a way of eating that includes Sweden, Denmark, and Norway. While each country's food culture is constantly evolving independently, Scandinavia's modern cuisines collectively focus on cooking at home with local, seasonal, and whole ingredients.

Ideally, a perfectly composed Scandinavian plate, reflecting the Nordic diet, would look something like this:

Vegetables and fruits occupy 50 percent of the plate. More vegetables than fruits, with a focus on variety—different colors, textures, and types.

Whole grains fill 25 percent of the plate. Variety is key, with an emphasis on rye, barley, oats, and other whole grains, while limiting white bread and white rice.

Healthy proteins make up the last 25 percent. Diverse and often plant-based protein sources include legumes, nuts, and seeds, though seafood remains a staple, particularly fatty fish such as sardines, salmon, and herring. Red meat and cheese are eaten in smaller portions, while processed meats like bacon, sausages, and lunch meats are avoided.

Additional beneficial components include canola and olive oil, nuts, and seeds, which add healthy fats and nutrients to meals.

For beverages, the Nordic diet encourages water, tea, or coffee. Milk, dairy products, and juice are consumed in moderation, while sugary drinks are avoided altogether. Alcohol is permitted in moderation.

A STOCKED KITCHEN

If you peeked into my pantry right now, you'd find shelves that feel like home to me—jars of grains lined up like old friends, tins of fish tucked away for a rainy day, and a few unexpected items, like mushroom garum or black garlic, waiting for their moment to shine. My fridge tells its own story, too, full of fresh essentials and little treasures that add more depth and flavor to my food.

For me, having a well-stocked kitchen isn't about being prepared for anything that comes my way. It's about creating possibilities and knowing that with the right ingredients and tools within reach, I can pull together a simple supper or something more special, even when I'm feeling uninspired. The ingredients in my pantry (and my fridge) are my ultimate safety net against the nuttiness of daily life. Cooking is a skill that one can practice, and it truly feels doable, almost second nature, when key basic ingredients are on hand. Here's my list of staples for your perusal:

OILS

There are always a few different bottles of oil in my kitchen. As a rule of thumb, I grab extra-virgin olive oil when making cold dressings or as a finishing oil, drizzled on the plated dish. Here in the United States, my go-to brand is California Olive Ranch, which has the perfect amount of grassy, buttery flavor and is made from 100 percent California olives.

When cooking with heat, I generally use a regular olive oil (not extra-virgin) because it's less assertive in flavor. I sometimes use it in dressings, too, replacing some or all of the extra-virgin, especially if I'm concerned that a strong olive flavor might mask the flavors of the other ingredients—as in the Pink Peppercorn Vinaigrette (page 55), for example.

Throughout this book, I sometimes call for a neutral oil, and in those instances you are free to use whichever lightest, least flavorful oil you prefer. Interestingly, the Nordic diet favors rapeseed (canola) oil as the oil of choice. It has a lot going for it: a neutral flavor, light texture, and a good amount of omega-3 fatty acids. Because much of the canola oil on the market is genetically modified, I stick with two non-GMO and organic brands: Spectrum and La Tourangelle.

La Tourangelle's canola oil is lovely, and it so happens they also make a roasted walnut oil that I always keep on hand. Not only does it impart a delicate earthiness to Walnut Vinaigrette (page 56), but it also works beautifully as a finishing oil, drizzled on vegetables or fish. I store it in the refrigerator to preserve its flavor and keep it from going rancid.

TINNED FISH

Jars of pickled herring—in a sugar-vinegar brine or creamy sauce—can be found in my refrigerator from time to time, but it's not something I regularly stock because I find an overstuffed fridge to often be more frustrating than inspiring. Instead, I prefer keeping a stack of shelf-stable tinned fish in the cupboard at all times. Whether the fish is spiced, smoked, or marinated in tomato sauce, chances are, I've got some. Packed with protein, omega-3s, and nutrients, tinned fish is not only good for you but incredibly satisfying and versatile.

The convenient size of each tin, paired with a few slices of crusty bread, makes for a perfect meal for one. And with a few cans, I'm set to make a double batch of Tinned Smoked Sardine Spread (page 70) as part of a stunning "seacuterie" board, together with shaved radish, cucumbers, dill sprigs, and rye crackers—it's my go-to spread to put out when dinner guests have arrived and I need a bit of time to finish preparing the meal.

When I shop for tinned fish, I reach first for small, abundant species like anchovies, sardines, or Atlantic (never King) mackerel. I'm especially fond of the Danish brand Fangst and their untraditional recipes, my favorite being smoked brisling—a.k.a. Baltic herring—prepared with heather and chamomile. To ensure the brand supports marine conservation programs that fish only safe species and use sound fishing methods, I always look for certifications from the Marine Stewardship Council or Friend of the Sea on the packaging.

If you are open to eating the skin and bones of the tinned fish, I salute you. Some people can get squeamish about it, but if you give it a try, you'll discover it's actually quite tasty and it isn't for nothing: The bones are rich in calcium, and the skin is full of omega-3s.

HERBS

Regardless of what you're cooking, the use of fresh herbs can truly enhance your food. A handful of fresh sprigs or a few spoonfuls of chopped herbs can add depth, brightness, and a sense of care to even the simplest dishes. In Scandinavian cooking, tender herbs like dill, parsley, chives, and tarragon are especially common. At Kantine, we stir a generous mix of all four, finely chopped, into softly scrambled eggs, a simple dish our guests often rave about.

Two herbs that I adore cooking with are lovage and sorrel. Lovage has a bold, herbaceous taste that reminds me of a cross between flat-leaf parsley and the pale inner leaves of a stalk of celery. It's often used in stews and soups, but I also love tossing a few sprigs into a pot of boiling new potatoes—its flavor subtly infuses the potatoes as they cook. Since I haven't had luck finding lovage in Northern California markets, I started growing a few plants on my back porch, and now I can't imagine my herb garden without them.

Sorrel is another favorite. As a kid, I called it sour grass. It has pretty heart-shaped leaves and tiny yellow flowers, both edible. I often toss it in green salads, and its lemony flavor lends itself particularly well to potato or egg preparations. There are many different varieties, but the one I use most often is wood sorrel, the type that grows wild in my backyard. If you can't find it at the grocer's, you might have more luck finding it in a green area nearby (see A Forager at Heart, page 239).

SPICES

I grew up in a home where the spices were always bought preground and had an endless shelf life, or so it seemed. My mom, who did most of the cooking, rarely used them, and so, it wasn't until I became an adult and started buying spices myself that I was struck by the magic of freshly ground, quality spices. My first eye-opening experience came when I started making spice blends for bacon I smoked in a Weber grill at home. From there, I began adding spices to my salt cures for salmon and trout, and then to the oil I slathered on top of a slab of bread dough before baking. Now, spices are essential in my kitchen—they add depth, flavor, and a sense of direction to my cooking.

My spice rack at home tends to be cramped, so to keep things manageable and maintain freshness (which I now know is so important!), I have narrowed it down to five essential spices to always have on hand: black peppercorns, paprika, sumac, cardamom, and madras curry. (If I run out of anything else, I don't buy it again until I need it.) Aside from kosher salt, these key spices provide a great foundation for everyday flavor. You'd be surprised how many different dishes can be made with them!

Likewise, we use a lot of spices at Kantine—the amount of cardamom seeds for our pastries alone are bought by the case, not jar. One spice company I'm especially fond of is Burlap & Barrel, which sources unique, beautiful spices and promotes heritage ingredients. Their Cured Sumac brings brightness to my Roasted Carrot Hummus (page 71), and their New Harvest Turmeric adds warmth to each batch of Mustard Curry Pickles (page 51).

SALT

Tried and true, kosher salt—specifically Diamond Crystal—has been in my life ever since I learned to cook. Other salts will work in a pinch (no pun intended!), but my fingertips have become so accustomed to the granule size of kosher that I have to exercise caution when using other types of salt to avoid oversalting. On occasions when I'm serving roast meat or fish on a platter, I'll switch to a flake salt, with its pretty pyramid crystals, giving the dish a delicate finishing touch.

SPROUTED RYE BREAD

Dark, seedy bread is a staple at Kantine, just as it is in my home. I adore its versatility—it can be toasted and slathered with butter and honey just as well as it can be topped with avocado and a fried egg. A few thin slices with toppings are my go-to lunch, a habit that was formed while living in Denmark. I promise you, it gives a feeling of fullness that you'll never get with white bread.

NUTS AND SEEDS

Birds know where it's at. Sprinkled on top of porridge, in salads, or just a handful as *kveldsmat* (a pre-bedtime snack), nuts and seeds are packed with flavor and texture, as well as nutrients like omega-3s, fiber, and protein. Spiced Crushed Nuts (page 43), a toasted nut trio (which you can customize), bring crunch to tender lettuce and herbs in the Butter Lettuce, Herb, and Nut Salad (page 127). Chocolate Muesli with Orange and Cashews (page 93) just wouldn't have the right "plump" texture without antioxidant-rich chia seeds. (To learn how to toast nuts and seeds, see page 42.)

BERRIES

Here in California, the local berry season is a heck of a lot longer than it is in Scandinavia, but even so, there are a few months when berries just don't taste of much. When berries are local and fresh, I buy them at the farmers' market. Most of the time they're eaten right away, but when they are at their prime, I stock up on even more, stowing a few bags in the freezer for Leftover Porridge Cakes with Cardamom, Skyr, and Crushed Red Berries (page 89) or Raspberry "Silk" with Dark Chocolate (page 256). Otherwise, the remainder of the juicy jewels are turned into jam, a thirst-quenching fruit-and-vinegar-based shrub, or lacto-fermented to blend into smoothies or salad dressings (see An Introduction to Lacto-Fermentation, page 50).

WHOLE GRAINS

Whole grains such as rye, barley, oats, and buckwheat bring texture and depth to hearty dishes, as in Barley Porridge with Spinach and Smoked Salmon (page 86) and Savory 3-Grain Porridge with Kale, Mushrooms, and Farmers Cheese (page 81). Rich in fiber, vitamins, and minerals, whole grains promote good gut health and provide steady energy.

I usually buy grains in the bulk department, and when it's time to cook them, I find it fun to mix and match—just keep in mind that grains may have different cooking times, so plan accordingly.

I find the term *whole grains* to be slightly misleading. It doesn't mean grains that are whole pieces but rather that 100 percent of the original kernel (which includes the bran, germ, and endosperm) is present. To better understand this, let's take barley. *Hulled* barley is a whole grain because it has all three parts intact (and only the inedible husk has been removed). However, *pearled* barley is not a whole grain because by "pearling" it, its husk *and* bran have been stripped away—resulting in a grain that is quicker to cook but also less nutritious. Therefore, flour can also be whole grain (even though it is ground) if it is made from whole grain kernels.

LEGUMES

Legumes are plants from the *Fabaceae* (or pea) family that produce fruit (in pods) and seeds used for food. Examples include lentils, split peas, and chickpeas. Legumes are extremely versatile, easy to cook, and nutritious. Personally, I love how satisfying they are: Even a small portion leaves me feeling nourished and content.

Legumes have been embraced in Scandinavian cuisines for some time, but they're even more commonplace now as a reliable source of protein, fiber, and nutrients like iron and folate in wholesome, plant-forward meals.

From traditional dishes like Swedish Yellow Pea Soup (page 173) to newer creations like Mung Bean Fritters with Goat Cheese (page 139) and 3-Lentil Hummus (page 66), I use them in so many different ways: simmered in soups and stews, pureed into spreads, or even sprouted for added crunch and nutrition. I often puree cooked legumes to "hide" them in sauces, soups, or mashed potatoes as a cunning way to boost nutrition, so my kids get the benefits without even noticing.

LIQUID AMINOS AND NUTRITIONAL YEAST

Both of these ingredients were introduced to me just a few years ago, and now I can't imagine not using them while cooking! What they have in common is that just a dash of either really adds oomph to your food, especially vegetarian preparations. Liquid aminos, which look and taste similar to soy sauce, deliver a salty, umami depth to soups, stews (like the Lemony Chickpea and Green Split Pea Stew, page 178), and marinades.

Nutritional yeast—nicknamed "nooch"—is a high-protein, nutrient-dense powdered seasoning that, like liquid aminos, imparts umami, but also a nutty, cheese-like flavor to dishes. I stir a few spoonfuls of it into the base for Mung Bean

Fritters with Goat Cheese (page 139), and it's also wonderful in a creamy dressing or sprinkled over roasted vegetables. One of my friends swears by sprinkling it on popcorn!

CHEESE

Scandinavia has long been a cheesemaking region, so it's no surprise that cheese has become central to many lunchtime spreads, often as a topping for open-faced sandwiches, and to many classic dishes. The Nordic diet encourages eating cheese in moderation, a guideline I can whole-heartedly adopt—I'd rather savor smaller amounts of great cheese than eat a larger amount of one that's just mediocre. Here are a few of my favorite go-to Scandinavian cheeses.

Västerbotten cheese is a sharp, nutty, hard cheese often referred to as the king of Swedish cheeses. It's notoriously hard to find in the United States, but I've found that Parmesan steps in beautifully, as I discovered once while making *Janssons frestelse,* the classic creamy potato gratin traditionally topped with Västerbotten. I didn't have any on hand, so I went with Parmesan instead. The result was slightly different, of course, but perfectly satisfying.

Whenever I'm at IKEA, I make sure to grab a few wedges of Swedish *Präst* cheese from the food market. Tangy and rich, with small holes and a flavor reminiscent of a baby Swiss, it's wonderful sliced thin on crispbread or rye.

For soft cheese, Danish Havarti is a crowd-pleaser. Mild, creamy, and beautifully meltable, it's hard not to like it. Here in San Francisco, my teenage son has become hooked on grilled Havarti sandwiches on sprouted rye bread. I jokingly tell him that the sandwiches are like him: a perfect mélange of Danish and American.

CULTURED DAIRY PRODUCTS

Cultured dairy products are integral to Scandinavian cooking, and I find myself using them for the cool tang and richness they add to my food. Here are the three I reach for time and time again:

Sour cream (*gräddfil* in Swedish) has the ability to become a beautiful base for cold sauces like Curry Cream (page 63), a dressing ingredient in Green Egg Salad (page 153), and a spreadable frosting for Smörgåstårta (Swedish Sandwich Cake, page 167). Often, I'll spoon it right from the container onto freshly boiled and still warm new potatoes with chives or swirl it into a hot bowl of soup.

Plain yogurt swings effortlessly between sweet and savory preparations. Some mornings, I like to stir it with fresh berries and granola. Other times, it becomes the base of a chilled sauce like Herbed Yogurt (page 60), ready to pair with just about anything—meat, fish, or a pile of roasted vegetables. My favorite is Straus's European-style plain yogurt: Its silky, rich texture and subtle tang make it a standout. (For more sauce inspiration, see A Cold Sauce Matrix, page 62.)

Filmjölk, or *fil* for short, is a Swedish cultured dairy product I first encountered when we had our summerhouse in Sweden. There, I'd use it instead of buttermilk, because we had no idea what buttermilk was called in Swedish, and by the time we found out, we'd already become too accustomed to the light, tender texture and tang that *fil* gave to our morning pancakes.

About a year ago I started making *fil* at home, using a culture I bought online. The process couldn't be easier, and even with 2 percent milk, the results are excellent. *Fil* has a looser consistency than regular yogurt, which can become the most lovely probiotic drink when blended with some fruit—it reminds me of a similar beverage enjoyed throughout Scandinavia.

PRESERVED LEMONS

Preserved lemons are not traditionally part of Scandinavian cuisine, but because of my fondness for lemons, they're always in my home kitchen. It's as if all the vibrant, sunny energy of their flesh and rinds is concentrated into something deeply savory, salty, and tangy. They bring complexity to grain salads and roasted vegetables and even add oomph to a simple, stirred cold sauce.

Many well-stocked grocery stores sell preserved lemons, but honestly, they're just as easy (and better) when made at home. You need only three ingredients: lemons, salt, and time (the measure, not the herb). Once preserved, they keep for months in the fridge. For a version I'm especially fond of, see the recipe for Preserved Spent Lemons (page 59), made from pre-juiced lemons.

PICKLED VEGETABLES

It seems like these days we're more aware of what makes food satisfying, delicious, and balanced. Traditional Scandinavian food, like many other cuisines, hasn't always been known for its vibrancy, but in recent years that has begun to change. One of the best ways I liven up a dish is with pickled vegetables. They're a brilliant way to make seasonal produce last longer, too. I could have filled half these pages with pickling recipes—once you tap into that world as I did years ago, you see the possibilities are endless. But to keep things simple—in true Scandinavian style—I've included only three of my tried-and-true recipes: Pickled Cucumbers (page 47), Pickled Red Onions (page 48), and Pickled Beets (page 48). To dip your toes into the subject, see Shelf-Stable Pickles (page 46), and for a deeper dive, I recommend grabbing a copy of Sandor Katz's indispensable *The Art of Fermentation* (2012).

ROOT VEGETABLES

Most of the root vegetables in my kitchen—sunchokes, carrots, parsnips—are only in need of a good scrub. It's a shame when more food than necessary ends up on the peeler, and then in the trash. The skins add fiber to our diet and leaving them on makes me feel better about reducing food waste. So at home, the rule is: shoes off at the door, skins on our veggies. It works most of the time. I keep two green scrubbies: one dedicated solely to scrubbing vegetables (and the occasional fruit), and another for dirty dishes. Of course, if the skin looks a little gnarly, it's probably best to peel it off.

LARDER

When I was a kid, my sister and I made a vinaigrette for the dinner salad every single night. We'd pour vinegar, water, and oil into a tall glass bottle marked with fill-to lines, then empty in the seasoning packet, close the lid, and shake. In our Italian American home, this was the only dressing we ever used.

A few years ago, my mom passed away, and when my siblings and I went to clean out the kitchen, we found the bottle and a packet of seasoning in the cupboard, waiting.

The best thing about a dressing like that was it was impossible to mess up. The recipe was virtually foolproof, yielding a flavorful dressing that had a good balance of acid and fat. Not only did we use it to dress green salads, but we would put it on pasta salads, marinate chicken in it, serve small ramekins of it alongside garlic bread for dipping, and stew pork in it. And although I have had my fill of that dressing for a lifetime, I can still appreciate foods that taste consistently good and are so eternally versatile. That's what this chapter aspires to offer you. It highlights a slew of easy-to-make recipes for spreads, dips, pulses, and dressings that I make time and again because they are hard to make taste bad and can be paired with practically anything else.

At any given time, I have a few different jars of these staples in my refrigerator at home, and a few more in the walk-in at Kantine. Frankly, having these staples an arm's length away allows me to enjoy cooking even more. I cook at home a lot, though sometimes I don't have much time to pull a meal together, and other times I feel simply uninspired, but I have learned that if I'm able to make just a few basic dishes—cooked grains, roasted vegetables, and/or a salad—my larder staples always do wonders to tie the meal together at the table.

As you work your way through the recipes in this chapter, you'll undoubtedly gain a better sense of basic Scandinavian ingredients, allowing you to connect dots to the rest of the recipes in this book and giving you an even deeper comprehension of the food of this region. (The sheer thought of that thrills me!) The sidebars are meant to offer more essential know-how and inspire other recipe ideas. With time, you'll be able to successfully swap ingredients from the original recipe with those that you already have in your kitchen, or with those that are in season where you live. In that way, this book grows with you. Suddenly, one recipe can become five, or possibly even more!

NUTS & SEEDS

4-Seed Sprinkle

Packed with healthy fats and protein, seeds get a green light in the Nordic diet. Yet my son won't let a single seed near his plate (a sure sign that he didn't take after me!). I like to throw this crunchy mix on just about everything, for more flavor and texture. A splash of liquid aminos brings out the nuttiness without making it entirely savory. This mix is delicious sprinkled on Shaved Melon and Spinach Salad with Feta (page 120) and Cauliflower Soup with Golden Garlic and Toasted Seeds (page 188), but I wouldn't hesitate to sprinkle it over my morning fruit and yogurt either. **MAKES 1 CUP**

½ cup (74 g) sunflower seeds

¼ cup (40 g) sesame seeds

2 tablespoons flaxseed

2 tablespoons pumpkin seeds

1½ teaspoons liquid aminos

1½ teaspoons neutral oil

Preheat the oven to 350°F (175°C). Line a baking tray with parchment paper.

In a small bowl, combine the sunflower seeds, sesame seeds, flaxseed, pumpkin seeds, liquid aminos, and oil, stirring until well combined. Pour onto the prepared baking tray and spread into an even layer. Bake, rotating the tray 180 degrees halfway through, until the seeds are lightly browned and fragrant, 16 to 20 minutes. Let cool completely. The seed mix will keep in an airtight container at room temperature for at least 2 weeks.

toasting nuts and seeds

Toasting nuts and seeds brings out their flavor and gives them a satisfying crunch. Since different nuts and seeds toast at different speeds, I always toast each type separately and then combine them afterward.

The two most common ways to toast nuts and seeds are in the oven and in a pan.

In the oven: Preheat the oven to 350°F (175°C). Spread the nuts or seeds into an even layer on a baking tray. Bake, stirring halfway through, until lightly browned and fragrant, 8 to 12 minutes.

In a pan: Heat a heavy dry skillet over medium heat. Add the nuts or seeds and stir frequently until lightly browned and fragrant, 3 to 5 minutes. Pour immediately into a bowl to cool.

Both methods work well, but each has its advantages. Oven toasting yields more even results inside and out, and is mostly hands-free, but it takes longer because you have to preheat the oven. Pan toasting is quicker, and I tend to use this method for small quantities, as my home oven has hot spots that cause small seeds like sesame to scorch in patches. Pan toasting requires my full attention, but if I continuously keep the seeds on the move, it's well worth the effort.

The cue I rely on most when toasting nuts and seeds is my sense of smell. That warm, nutty, toasty aroma is the best sign that they're perfectly done.

No matter which method you use, let the nuts and seeds cool completely on a baking tray before storing them in an airtight container. They'll keep at room temperature for at least 2 weeks.

Spiced Crushed Nuts

The irresistible crunch of these nuts comes from the spiced egg white the nuts are coated with prior to being baked. Let them rain down on a leafy green salad, like the ravishing Butter Lettuce, Herb, and Nut Salad (page 127), or a grated root vegetable slaw. I prefer to use whole nuts (with the exception of walnuts) and crush them with the side of a knife or kitchen mallet so they vary in size and feel more organic in shape than presliced pieces. I use walnuts, almonds, and hazelnuts in this recipe, but I have yet to find a nut combination that doesn't work, so feel free to use your favorites instead! **MAKES 1 CUP**

Neutral oil, for greasing

⅓ cup (30 g) walnut pieces

⅓ cup (50 g) whole almonds

⅓ cup (43 g) whole hazelnuts

1 teaspoon juniper berries

½ teaspoon caraway seeds

2 teaspoons coriander seeds

1 teaspoon anise seeds

2 teaspoons fennel seeds

1 egg white, lightly whisked

¼ teaspoon kosher salt

Preheat the oven to 350°F (175°C). Grease a baking tray with a touch of oil.

Place all the nuts on a large cutting board and, with your palm pressing down on the broad side of a chef's knife, crush the nuts into irregular pieces, leaving no nuts whole.

In a spice grinder or mortar, grind the juniper berries to small bits, like coarse-ground black pepper. (Juniper is especially pungent when eaten in larger pieces, so grinding it before the other spices ensures it's small enough.)

Add the caraway, coriander, anise, and fennel seeds to the grinder or mortar and grind until coarsely ground.

In a small bowl, stir together the egg white, ground spices, salt, and the crushed nuts. Pour onto the prepared baking tray and spread into an even layer. Bake, stirring the mixture and rotating the tray halfway through, until golden brown, 20 to 25 minutes. Let cool completely, break it up, then store in an airtight container for up to 2 weeks.

4-Seed Sprinkle

Spiced Crushed Nuts

PICKLES & PRESERVES

MUSTARD CURRY PICKLES
WIDE MOUTH
PICKLED BEETS
WIDE MOUTH

One surefire way to make seasonal produce last longer is to preserve it with pickling. Pickling doesn't always have to involve vinegar and sugar, but it's the most common method in Scandinavia. As daunting as it may seem, pickling isn't difficult. Quick pickles, like the ones in this chapter, can be made and refrigerated immediately. If your goal is to make a larger batch to store at room temperature, canning requires a few extra steps, but it's quite straightforward, too.

If you'd like to get a better idea of what produce is in its prime in your area, I recommend checking out the FoodPrint's Seasonal Food Guide, an online national database of produce availability here in the United States. All you have to do is put in your state to get a great overview of what grows when.

Glass mason jars are my containers of choice for pickles. I like that the glass makes it easy to see what's inside, they're easy to clean (especially the wide-mouthed kind), and they help reduce the amount of plastic being used in the kitchen.

QUICK PICKLES FOR THE REFRIGERATOR

When making quick pickles, simply prepare your brine, pack the jars with vegetables, and pour the brine over them to fill the jars. Let them cool to room temperature before putting on the lids, then refrigerate. They'll be ready to eat in a day or two, and once opened, they should be eaten within 4 weeks. Unopened, they typically keep for 1 to 2 months.

SHELF-STABLE PICKLES

If your batch is big and/or your refrigerator space is too precious, canning your pickles for room-temperature shelf storage can save a lot of valuable refrigerator space. The first step is to sterilize the jars. To do so, bring a big pot of water to a boil, remove the jar lids, and lower both the jars and lids into the boiling water. If your pot isn't big enough, work in batches. Boil for 10 minutes, then carefully remove the jars with tongs, pouring out any water inside. Set them right side up on the counter to air-dry—no dish towels (which can reintroduce bacteria).

The second step is to fill your jars with vegetables and brine just as you would with quick pickles. Then, with lids on, lower the jars into a large pot of boiling water, making sure they're fully submerged with at least 1 inch (2.5 cm) of water above the lids. Boil for 10 to 15 minutes, then carefully remove them with tongs and let them cool at room temperature. As the jars cool, the lids will seal (you'll hear a pop), telling you that they now are ready to be stored in a cool, dark place for up to 3 months. Once the jar's seal has been broken, the jar will have to be stored in the refrigerator and will keep for up to 4 weeks.

Note

For non-pickled, low-acid food canning projects with vegetables, meats, or soups, you will need to use a pressure canner to ensure your food stays safe. Though I fully support maintaining a plentiful larder, pressure canning is a process I don't work with often, so I encourage you to explore trusted resources on the subject.

The Most Basic Pickling Brine

I'm a fan of this basic brine for vegetables because it is not so in-your-face vinegary and allows the vegetable flavor to shine through. Think of it as a starting point, where whole spices like mustard seeds or coriander, fresh herbs like dill or tarragon, or aromatics like garlic, ginger, or dried chiles can be added for extra flavor.

This batch size will be enough to pickle about 2 pounds (900 g) of prepared vegetables, though that amount can vary depending on how the vegetables are cut and how much they compress in the brine. **MAKES 1 QUART**

- 2 cups (480 g) water
- 2 cups (480 g) vinegar (white or apple cider)
- 2 tablespoons kosher salt
- 1 tablespoon sugar (optional)

In a small saucepan, bring all the ingredients to a boil. Remove from the heat and give the mixture a quick stir to help dissolve the sugar, if using. If you are pickling waxy vegetables like green beans or peppers, pour the brine over the vegetables hot. With more delicate vegetables like cucumbers and onions, let the brine cool to room temperature before pouring it over the vegetables.

Pickled Cucumbers

In Denmark, quick-pickled cucumbers are a classic hot dog topping, as well as a garnish for open-faced liver pâté sandwiches. I like using English cucumbers for their thinner skin and fewer seeds, but any crisp variety will do. Once they're ready, use them to make Danish Remoulade (page 60) or serve them alongside Vegetable and Bean Hash (page 208) as a lively condiment. I read somewhere that drinking pickle juice is good for you, too, just in case your desire to reduce food waste has you sneaking sips of the brine straight from the jar. **MAKES 1½ QUARTS**

BRINE

- 3 cups (720 g) white vinegar
- 2½ cups (500 g) sugar
- ½ cup (80 g) kosher salt
- 1 teaspoon mustard seeds
- 1 bay leaf

- 2 pounds (900 g) cucumbers, preferably English, cut into ⅛- to ¼-inch (3 to 6 mm) slices
- 2 sprigs of dill
- 2 sprigs of tarragon

Make the brine. In a medium pot, combine the vinegar, sugar, salt, mustard seeds, and bay leaf and bring to a boil over medium-high heat. Remove from the heat and give the mixture a quick stir to help dissolve the sugar. Let cool to room temperature.

Meanwhile, put the cucumber slices, dill, and tarragon into your preferred container—either an airtight container or mason jars.

Strain the brine through a fine-mesh sieve to remove the whole spices, then pour the brine over the cucumbers. Place a small round of parchment paper directly on the surface to help keep the pickles submerged. Place a lid on the container and refrigerate.

The pickles can be eaten after just a few days but taste even better after a week. Store in the refrigerator and use within 4 weeks. If you'd like to can the pickles instead, be sure to read Shelf-Stable Pickles (page 46) before getting started.

Pickled Red Onions

This recipe appeared in my first book, *Scandinavian from Scratch,* but I wanted to include it here as well, since I find these onions indispensable. They add a sharp, tangy bite to just about anything, from sandwiches to grain bowls, and they pair so well with a cool, creamy sauce, too. There's no brine to prepare in advance, so these are a cinch to make. Some red onions are more pigmented than others, so I like to tuck in a slice of raw beet while the onions are macerating in the vinegar to guarantee a vibrant magenta color. **MAKES 1 CUP**

1 large red onion (8 ounces / 225 g), halved and sliced into ¼-inch (6 mm) strips

1 tablespoon kosher salt

1 small slice of red beet (optional)

½ cup (116 g) red wine vinegar, plus more as needed

Place the onion in a nonreactive (glass or stainless-steel) bowl and sprinkle with the salt. Stir together and let sit until the onion is limp, about 15 minutes. Add the beet slice, if using, then pour enough vinegar to come halfway up the onion slices. Let the mixture sit for about 1 hour, giving it a stir every 10 to 15 minutes. At this point the onions can be used right away or the mixture can be transferred to an airtight container and stored in the refrigerator for up to 2 weeks.

Pickled Beets

These beets are bright, punchy, and, thanks to the horseradish, ready to liven up just about anything. Leftover beet brine can be repurposed, too. Whisk it into salad dressings, add it to marinades, or use it to dye the exterior of hard-boiled eggs a gorgeous shade of pink (opposite). Try these beets atop Vegetarian Mushroom Pâté (page 160) and as a condiment for Beef Kalops Stew (page 211) or Vegetable and Bean Hash (page 208). **MAKES 3 CUPS**

1 pound (454 g) red beets, trimmed (golden and Chioggia beets work just as well)

BRINE

1½ cups (360 g) white vinegar

½ cup plus 2 tablespoons (125 g) sugar

2 cardamom pods

½ cinnamon stick

3 whole allspice berries

Place the beets in a medium pot and add a pinch of salt and cold water to cover by about 1 inch (2.5 cm). Bring to a boil over high heat, then decrease the heat to low and simmer for 20 to 40 minutes, depending on the size of the beets. Test for doneness with a fork. They should be tender in the middle like boiled potatoes. As they finish cooking, you may see their skins slipping off. Drain them in a colander and rinse under cold water, removing any remaining skin. Set aside to cool.

While the beets cool, make the brine. In a medium pot, combine the vinegar, sugar, cardamom, cinnamon, allspice, bay leaves, mustard seeds, peppercorns, salt, and thyme and bring to a boil over high heat. Remove from the heat and give the mixture a quick stir to help dissolve the sugar. Let cool to room temperature.

When the beets have cooled, cut them into chunks or thick slices and put into your preferred container—either an airtight container or mason jars.

Strain the brine through a fine-mesh sieve to remove the whole spices, then pour it over the beets. Top with sliced horseradish. Place a lid on the container and refrigerate.

The beets can be eaten after just a few days but taste even better after a week. Store in the refrigerator and use within 4 weeks. If you'd like to can the beets instead, be sure to read Shelf-Stable Pickles (page 46) before getting started.

2 bay leaves

1 teaspoon mustard seeds

1 teaspoon black peppercorns

1 teaspoon kosher salt, plus more for cooking the beets

5 sprigs of thyme

2 ounces (56 g) fresh horseradish, peeled and thinly sliced

an introduction to lacto-fermentation

Some years ago, a light bulb went off for me, an almost mind-blowing realization that so many of our fruits and vegetables could be fermented, transforming them into something familiar yet entirely different, thanks to the work of lactic acid bacteria.

Now, don't let the idea of bacteria in your food make you squeamish. Whether you like it or not, bacteria are there naturally. But in the right environment, different bacteria can convert sweet to sour, simple to complex; they give Danish rye bread, beer, and pickles their characteristic tang. What's even more amazing is that fermentation also gives new life to foods that might otherwise end up in the bin, like cauliflower cores and watermelon rinds.

Lacto-fermentation is one of the oldest and simplest ways to preserve produce, using nothing more than salt and time. This process encourages the growth of these powerful bacteria while keeping food safe and full of beneficial probiotics.

The method is straightforward. The standard ratio for a brine is 2 percent salt by weight. That means for every 1,000 grams of produce, you'll add 20 grams of salt. If you are fermenting whole or large pieces of vegetables, like carrots or cucumbers, you'll need to mix the salt with water to create an oxygen-free environment, which helps safeguard the ingredients from contamination. However, if you are fermenting shredded vegetables, like cabbage for sauerkraut, massaging them with salt until they release enough of their own juices to submerge themselves is enough.

At Kantine, we often lacto-ferment fruits—like berries, pears, and apples—as a way to enhance their natural sweetness with a bit of contrasting saltiness. Recently I made a small batch of lacto-fermented strawberries at home. Once they were ready, I stirred in an equal amount of fresh, unfermented strawberries and spooned the mix over my morning porridge. The result was such a surprise: The texture of the fermented berries was firmer and plump, and the flavor was concentrated, a little salty and very fruity—utterly delicious!

Fermentation time can range from a few days to a few weeks, depending on temperature and other factors. Keep an eye on your fermentation and taste it when you think it might be ready, then move it to the refrigerator to keep your goods from getting a bit too funky. For more on the subject, I highly recommend *The Noma Guide to Fermentation* (2018) by René Redzepi and David Zilber. It's a fantastic read with down-to-earth explanations and inspiring recipes.

Mustard Curry Pickles

These pickles are a little unusual in that the vegetables aren't preserved in a brine but rather in a thick, punchy sauce made with mustard, curry, vinegar, and sugar. When finely chopped, they can be stirred into a mayonnaise base to create Danish Remoulade (page 60), the classic condiment for fish cakes, open-faced sandwiches, and Danish hot dogs. Traditionally the sauce is thickened with flour, but I prefer using cornstarch to make the recipe gluten-free. Similar to British piccalilli, these pickles are a wonderful way to use up an abundance of seasonal vegetables. In the warmer months, I reach for green beans and zucchini, and when it's cold, I turn to cabbage, brussels sprouts, or broccoli. You can swap vegetables freely, as long as the overall weight remains the same. **MAKES 2 QUARTS**

8 ounces (224 g) carrots, scrubbed and cut into 1-inch (2.5 cm) chunks

8 ounces (224 g) cauliflower florets, cut into bite-size pieces

6 ounces (168 g) celery root, peeled and cut into 1-inch (2.5 cm) chunks

6 ounces (168 g) yellow onion, cut into 1-inch (2.5 cm) chunks

5 ounces (140 g) English cucumber, cut lengthwise, seeded, and cut into bite-size pieces

4 ounces (112 g) parsnip, scrubbed and cut into 1-inch (2.5 cm) chunks

3 ounces (84 g) green beans, snipped and cut into bite-size segments

Kosher salt

4 cups (960 g) white vinegar

1⅓ cups (320 g) sugar

3 bay leaves

⅓ cup (45 g) cornstarch

3 tablespoons madras curry powder

½ teaspoon chili powder

3 tablespoons mustard powder

2 tablespoons mustard seeds

1 tablespoon sweet paprika

1 tablespoon ground turmeric

½ cup (120 g) cold water

In a large bowl, combine the carrots, cauliflower, celery root, onion, cucumber, parsnip, green beans, and 2 tablespoons salt. Toss to combine, then cover and leave at room temperature for 4 hours or overnight in the refrigerator.

Fill a large pot with water and bring to a boil over high heat. Rinse the salted vegetables in cold water and then add about half to the boiling water. Cook until the carrots are just cooked through, about 3 minutes. Use a slotted spoon or spider to scoop the vegetables out onto a baking tray, spreading them into an even layer so they can cool. Repeat with the remaining vegetables. Once all the vegetables cool to room temperature, put them into your preferred container—either an airtight container or mason jars.

While the vegetables cool, start the sauce. Wipe out the pot and add the vinegar, sugar, bay leaves, chile, and a pinch of salt. Bring to a boil over high heat.

In a small bowl, stir together the cornstarch, curry powder, chili powder, mustard powder, mustard seeds, paprika, turmeric, cold water, and a pinch of salt. Pour the spice mixture into the boiling liquid and whisk until it has returned to a boil and thickened. Ladle the sauce over the vegetables, sticking a butter knife down along the jar sides to move the vegetables, allowing the sauce to reach all parts of each jar. The sauce should cover the top as well. Immediately top the jars with the lids and refrigerate.

The pickles can be eaten after just a few days but taste even better after a week. Use within 4 weeks. If you'd like to can the mustard curry pickles instead, be sure to read Shelf-Stable Pickles (page 46) before getting started.

DRESSINGS & SAUCES

SAFFRON VIN
preserved lemon
vinaigrette
WALNUT VIN

Basic Vinaigrette

A good vinaigrette is one of those things that often goes unnoticed—that is, until it's missing. Acidity, sweetness, and salt suspended in oil. I debated whether to include a recipe this basic, but its simplicity is exactly what makes it universal. I let the shallots macerate in vinegar to soften their sharpness. I find it convenient to shake everything together in a mason jar so that whatever doesn't get used this time around can just be lidded and refrigerated until next time. **MAKES 1 CUP**

¼ cup (60 g) white wine vinegar, plus more as needed

1 tablespoon minced shallot

½ cup (110 g) extra-virgin olive oil

1½ teaspoons runny honey, plus more as needed

1 teaspoon Dijon mustard

Kosher salt and freshly ground black pepper

In a jar with a tight-fitting lid, combine the vinegar and shallot and set aside for 15 minutes to macerate. Add the olive oil, honey, and mustard with a pinch of salt and pepper. Cover and shake vigorously until emulsified. Taste and season with more salt, vinegar, or honey, if needed. (Alternatively, make the dressing using a bowl and whisk, whisking the oil in slowly at the end until the mixture emulsifies.) The vinaigrette can be made in advance and stored in an airtight container in the refrigerator for up to 7 days.

Saffron Vinaigrette

There's something magical about saffron—maybe that's why it shows up in so many different cuisines. In Sweden, it's prominent in baking, especially during the holidays, when a sense of luxury and celebration fills the air. But in this recipe, saffron shows off its ability to transform savory foods too. As much as I love seeing those vivid golden threads in food, I gently crush them before blooming to unlock more of their gorgeous color. **MAKES 1 CUP**

½ teaspoon (about 50 threads) saffron

¼ cup (60 g) champagne or white wine vinegar, plus more as needed

1 tablespoon minced shallot

½ cup (110 g) olive oil

2 teaspoons fresh lemon juice, plus more as needed

1½ teaspoons runny honey, plus more as needed

1 teaspoon Dijon mustard

Kosher salt and freshly ground black pepper

Using your fingers, crush the saffron into small pieces over a small bowl or measuring cup so you don't lose any. This will make the saffron flavor even more prevalent, while keeping some pretty orange flecks.

Bring a small amount of water to a boil (I do it in the microwave) and spoon 1 tablespoon of boiling water over the saffron. Allow it to steep for at least 30 minutes, but if possible, for a few hours.

In a jar with a tight-fitting lid, combine the vinegar and shallot and set aside for 15 minutes to macerate. Add the olive oil, lemon juice, honey, mustard, steeped saffron and saffron water, and a pinch of salt and pepper. Cover and shake vigorously until emulsified. Taste and season with more salt, vinegar, lemon, or honey, if needed. (Alternatively, make the dressing using a bowl and whisk, whisking the oil in slowly at the end until the mixture emulsifies.) The vinaigrette can be made in advance and stored in an airtight container in the refrigerator for up to 7 days.

Pink Peppercorn Vinaigrette

The first time I used pink peppercorns was in culinary school in the '90s. Back then, the small pink pearls were all the rage, touted as the sassy sister to black peppercorns, showing up in dishes like pink peppercorn–crusted salmon and filet mignon with pink peppercorn sauce. But then came the scandal: Pink and black peppercorns aren't even from the same family! And then just like that, pink peppercorns lost their novelty and disappeared for years. It wasn't until just recently that they started popping up in recipes again (this one included), for the bright, oily, almost piney quality they bring to food. Speaking of bright, Spring's Sun (page 102) is the perfect place for this vinaigrette to shine. **MAKES 1 CUP**

- 3 tablespoons apple cider vinegar
- 1 tablespoon minced shallot
- ¼ cup (55 g) extra-virgin olive oil
- ¼ cup (55 g) neutral oil
- 1 tablespoon Dijon mustard
- 2 teaspoons pink peppercorns, lightly crushed
- ¼ teaspoon sugar
- Kosher salt and freshly ground black pepper
- 2 tablespoons chopped fresh flat-leaf parsley
- 1 tablespoon chopped fresh tarragon
- 1 tablespoon chopped fresh chives

In a jar with a tight-fitting lid, combine the vinegar and shallot and set aside for 15 minutes to macerate. Add the oils, mustard, pink peppercorns, and sugar. Cover and shake vigorously until emulsified. (Alternatively, make the dressing using a bowl and whisk, whisking the oil in slowly at the end until the mixture emulsifies.) Season with salt and black pepper, then stir in the herbs. The vinaigrette can be made in advance and stored in an airtight container in the refrigerator for up to 1 day. (The herbs don't allow this vinaigrette to be stored for a longer period.)

VARIATION

Egg and Pink Peppercorn Vinaigrette

This version takes inspiration from *gribiche,* a classic French sauce made with hard-boiled eggs, mustard, and pickles, usually whisked into an emulsified dressing. Mine is looser, less structured, and free of pickles, allowing the pink peppercorns to shine. It's terrific to spoon over potatoes, asparagus, sunchokes, or artichokes.

- 2 hard-boiled eggs (see Perfect Hard-Boiled Eggs, page 154)

Peel and cut each egg into eighths. Gently stir into the dressing just before serving.

Walnut Vinaigrette

Every time I reach for the walnuts in my freezer, I think of my mom, who taught me to store them there to keep them fresh longer. I do the same with walnut oil, tucking it into the fridge so it doesn't turn rancid. This walnut-y vinaigrette is a personal favorite, especially in the Kale and Einkorn Salad with Mirabelles (page 119). I adore the way the sweetness of the walnuts and golden balsamic vinegar—a balsamic made with white grapes that has a crispier and fruitier taste than traditional balsamic—pairs with the bitterness of the kale, but it works just as well on roasted vegetables or a hearty grain salad. If you have trouble getting your hands on golden balsamic vinegar, sherry vinegar is another great option that adds a deeper, slightly caramelized flavor. Since the vinaigrette keeps for up to 2 weeks, I always make extra. **MAKES 1½ CUPS**

- ¼ cup (60 g) golden or white balsamic vinegar
- ¼ cup (35 g) minced shallots
- ½ cup (110 g) neutral oil
- ¼ cup (55 g) walnut oil
- ⅔ cup (58 g) toasted walnut pieces, coarsely chopped (see Toasting Nuts and Seeds, page 42)
- Kosher salt and freshly ground black pepper
- Fresh lemon juice, for serving

In a jar with a tight-fitting lid, combine the vinegar and shallots and set aside for 15 minutes to macerate. Add the oils and walnuts, cover, and shake vigorously until emulsified. (Alternatively, make the dressing using a bowl and whisk, whisking the oil in slowly at the end until the mixture emulsifies.) Season with salt and pepper. I like to have some lemon juice on hand to sprinkle on and brighten up the food you are dressing just before serving. The dressing can be made in advance and stored in an airtight container in the refrigerator for up to 2 weeks.

Mormor Dressing

In Danish, *mormor* means "grandmother" or "grandma," and this dressing's name was already coined by someone else, I suspect as a nod to the simple, comforting flavors of traditional home cooking. My friend Malene's grandmother used to invite us over for lunch often, and despite being in her nineties, she was able to prepare a wonderful meal, where tender baby greens were tossed in this dressing. The acidity thickens the cream slightly, creating a light, tangy coating that clings to lettuce, as in the Butter Lettuce, Herb, and Nut Salad (page 127), without feeling heavy. It is most likely one of the easiest creamy dressings you'll ever make. **MAKES ⅓ CUP**

- 1 tablespoon fresh lemon juice
- ½ teaspoon sugar
- Pinch of kosher salt
- Freshly ground black pepper
- ⅓ cup (80 g) heavy cream

In a medium bowl, stir together the lemon juice, sugar, and salt until the sugar is dissolved. Add a few grinds of black pepper. Pour in the cream and whisk lightly until thickened slightly. The ideal consistency is thin enough to drizzle and coat a lettuce leaf, but without clumping. If the dressing is too thick, add a drop or two of water. Dress your greens and serve immediately. The dressing can be stored in an airtight container in the refrigerator for 1 day, but for best results, make it just before you need it.

Garlic Anchovy Dressing

This dressing is another great way to put tinned fish to use. Funnily enough, what Swedes call *ansjovis* is often translated as "anchovies" in English, but it's actually an entirely different fish: sprats! So, to be crystal clear, we're using the small, oily anchovies found at most US grocery stores for this recipe. (And if you're after a truly exceptional anchovy, I highly recommend the Cantabrian anchovies from Fishwife—dangerously good!)

Inspired by the sauce bagna càuda, this dressing's umami-rich ingredients bring earthy and rich flavors to the Celery Root, Kale, and Parsley Salad with Spiced Breadcrumbs (page 105). The garlic is briefly boiled to soften its sharpness, then slowly simmered with the anchovies in olive oil until everything melds into one deeply savory base. Once the oil has cooled, vinegar, lemon juice, and a pinch of red pepper flakes make the dressing complete. Just a warning, go easy on adding any additional salt, since the anchovies are fairly salty to start. **MAKES 1 CUP**

- 10 to 12 garlic cloves (about 30 g), peeled
- ½ cup (110 g) extra-virgin olive oil
- ¼ cup (50 g) anchovy fillets in oil (about 15 fillets), coarsely chopped
- 5 teaspoons red wine vinegar
- Finely grated zest of ½ lemon
- 5 teaspoons fresh lemon juice
- ½ teaspoon crushed red pepper flakes
- Kosher salt and freshly ground black pepper

Place the garlic in a small saucepan with water to cover. Bring to a gentle simmer over medium heat and cook, stirring occasionally, until tender, about 5 minutes. Drain and return the garlic to the same pan.

Over medium heat, cook off any residual moisture in the pan and, when dry, add the olive oil. Decrease the heat to low and add the anchovies. Simmer the mixture gently, using a fork to mash the garlic and anchovies into a paste as they cook, about 5 minutes.

Pour the warm mixture into a medium bowl and let cool to room temperature. Whisk in the vinegar, lemon zest and juice, and red pepper flakes. Taste and season with salt and pepper but be careful to not add too much salt. The dressing can be made in advance and stored in an airtight container in the refrigerator for 1 week.

Preserved Lemon Vinaigrette

Throughout this book, I call for fresh lemon juice because it has a vibrancy and clean flavor that bottled lemon juice just can't match. Bottled juice would be a last resort if lemons weren't available, mainly because it's typically pasteurized to extend its shelf life, but at the cost of losing much of its zesty ping. My favorite zero-waste way to use up those peels after squeezing out all the juice is to make a batch of Preserved Spent Lemons (page 59). This vinaigrette is a marriage of both fresh and preserved lemon—the salty, fermented peel of the preserved lemons gives this dressing complexity, the fresh juice adds mouth-puckering sourness, and the honey takes off the edge. It's a wonderful example of ingredients working in harmony to achieve balance, as it does in the Roasted Sunchokes with Dandelion Greens, Almonds, and Rye Crackers (page 131). Try adding poppy seeds to add a pretty detail to lighter-colored salads. **MAKES ¾ CUP**

- 1 Preserved Spent Lemon (2 halves; page 59) or store-bought preserved lemon
- 2½ tablespoons golden or white balsamic vinegar
- 2 tablespoons fresh lemon juice
- 1 teaspoon runny honey
- ½ teaspoon minced garlic
- ⅓ cup (73 g) extra-virgin olive oil
- Kosher salt and freshly ground black pepper
- 1 tablespoon poppy seeds (optional)

With a paring knife, scrape the preserved lemon peel clean, discarding the innards. Rinse the peel in cold water and chop it coarsely. Place the peel in a blender with the vinegar, lemon juice, honey, and garlic and blend everything together into a thick puree. Scrape down the sides of the blender, then cover it and, with the blender running on medium speed, slowly add the oil through the top. Taste and season with salt and pepper, although it might not need any salt at all. (The vinaigrette can also be made in a mortar with a pestle.) Stir in the poppy seeds, if desired. It can be made in advance and stored in an airtight container in the refrigerator for up to 1 week.

preserved spent lemons

In my humble opinion, lemons are sassy and sexy, and they can brighten up most any dish. At Kantine, we go through a lot of lemons, and I struggle with seeing any part of the fruit go to waste. Even after juicing, there's still so much flavor left in the peels—the essential oils, the bit of juice that refuses to be squeezed out. Instead of tossing them, we coat them with salt and pack them into mason jars. Over a few weeks, the peels soften, the flavors deepen, and what was once just "leftovers" transforms into something intensely lemony, but in a beautifully complex way.

Traditional preserved lemons are made with whole fruit (Ottolenghi's method is a favorite), but I love this zero-waste approach. It's especially easy to do in big batches when lemons are particularly juicy (and cheaper than usual). Once preserved, the peels can be chopped and added to dressings, stews, and braises, while the salty, lemon-infused brine becomes a secret weapon in vinaigrettes and marinades.

While this version sticks to just lemons and salt, I've heard wonderful stories of people preserving them with chiles, spices, and herbs. It's on my culinary to-do list, but for now, I'm happy knowing that every last bit of these lemons has been put to good use. MAKES 8 TO 10 PRESERVED LEMONS

8 to 10 whole organic lemons

1 cup (135 g) kosher salt

Extra-virgin olive oil, for storage

Sterilize a 1-quart (1L) mason jar. See instructions in Shelf-Stable Pickles (page 46).

Wash the lemons, cut them in half crosswise, and juice them using a lemon reamer or juicer. Refrigerate or freeze the juice for use in other recipes. If you are working with juiced, leftover rind halves, you can skip this step.

In a large bowl, toss the lemon peels with the salt. Pack the salted peels tightly together into the prepared mason jar, pressing them down firmly. Pour any salt remaining in the bowl into the jar, put a lid on the jar, and leave it at room temperature for about 1 week.

When you notice the lemons begin to soften, use a spoon to press down firmly and compress them further. Add enough boiled and cooled water (this sterilizes it) to the jar to bring the liquid level to just cover the lemons and then cover with a thin layer of olive oil. Seal the jar and leave for at least 3 weeks. Once the peels have turned translucent, they're ready to use. Move the jar to the refrigerator for long-term storage. The peels will continue to develop flavor over time, up to 1 year in the refrigerator. Before using, rinse the preserved peels thoroughly in cold water, as the saltiness can be intense.

Danish Remoulade

My friend Henrik has a deep love for Danish remoulade—I've never seen anyone pile it so enthusiastically onto slice after slice of rye bread. If we ran out of bread, he might just continue eating it with a spoon. Unlike its French counterpart, which skips the pickled vegetables, the Danish version is boldly yellow thanks to turmeric (see photograph, opposite). The color intensifies as it sits, making it even more vibrant by the time you're ready to dig in. While homemade Mustard Curry Pickles (page 51) or Pickled Cucumbers (page 47) are ideal components to make remoulade with, you can substitute store-bought British piccalilli and cornichons if needed. **MAKES 2 CUPS**

- ½ cup (125 g) Mustard Curry Pickles (page 51), including sauce, finely chopped
- ½ cup (90 g) Pickled Cucumbers (page 47), finely chopped
- ½ cup (100 g) mayonnaise
- ¼ cup (63 g) sour cream
- 1 tablespoon capers, rinsed in cold water, finely chopped
- 2 sprigs of tarragon, leaves finely chopped
- ½ teaspoon ground turmeric
- Pinch of madras curry powder
- Kosher salt and freshly ground black pepper

In a medium bowl, stir together the curry pickles, pickled cucumbers, mayonnaise, sour cream, capers, tarragon, turmeric, and curry powder. Season with salt and pepper. The remoulade can be made in advance and stored in an airtight container in the refrigerator for up to 5 days.

Herbed Yogurt

Cool and creamy, this yogurt is lovely to dip pieces of Carrot Sheet Pan Bread (page 240) into as a snack, and as a cold sauce for Oat and Sunflower Seed Cakes (page 150). **MAKES 1 CUP**

- 1 cup (250 g) plain whole milk yogurt (not Greek yogurt)
- 3 sprigs of dill, stemmed and leaves chopped
- 6 fresh chives, thinly sliced
- 1 tablespoon minced shallot
- Kosher salt and freshly ground black pepper

In a medium bowl, stir together the yogurt, dill, chives, and shallot until well combined. Season with salt and pepper. The yogurt can be made in advance and stored in an airtight container in the refrigerator for up to 5 days.

a cold sauce matrix

Cold sauces bring balance, richness, and contrast to a dish. They can round out the saltiness of cured fish, add a zing to roasted meats, or turn a simple sandwich into something special. Thankfully, they come together quickly and can be easily adjusted based on what's in your kitchen. Two examples included here are Curry Cream (page 63) and Herbed Yogurt (page 60), but here's a mix-and-match guide to help you create your own cold sauces. The rules are simple: Choose at least one ingredient from each category and whisk together, adjusting to taste.

1 base

builds the foundation

plain european-style yogurt or skyr
thick, tangy, and protein-rich

crème fraîche or sour cream
cool and velvety with a touch of acidity

mayonnaise
rich and creamy, perfect for spreading on a sandwich

buttermilk or *filmjölk*
thin, tart, and great for drizzling (see more on filmjölk in Honey Toasted Sesame Oats with Filmjölk and Watermelon, page 90)

2 acid

adds brightness

lemon juice
classic and bright

apple cider vinegar
sharp with depth

pickled beet brine
salty and full of character (see Pickled Beets, page 48)

dijon or grainy mustard
a little spice and bite

3 fat

brings a silky depth

extra-virgin olive oil
grassy with a buttery flavor

brown butter
nutty, sweet caramelization

curry oil
warm and tantalizing

tahini
earthy and slightly bitter

4 flavor boost

adds complexity

grated horseradish
peppery and sharp

minced fresh garlic
a little goes a long way

roasted garlic or black garlic paste
deep and molasses-like

chopped capers
salty and briny

chopped soft herbs
the more the merrier (my favorites are tarragon and dill)

minced preserved lemon
salty brightness (see Preserved Spent Lemons, page 59)

mashed anchovies
deeply savory with a hint of funk

toasted sesame seeds
oily and delicate (see Toasting Nuts and Seeds, page 42)

Curry Cream

Curry might not be the first thing you associate with Scandinavian cooking, but it found its way into the region's kitchens in the 1900s, especially in Denmark. Dishes like *boller i karry* (meatballs in curry sauce) and *karrysild* (curried herring) feature mild spice blends suited to local palates. (Mustard Curry Pickles, page 51, is another example.) Here, curry powder is gently heated in neutral oil to release its aromatics and deepen the flavor. That golden oil is then stirred into a creamy base with a squeeze of lemon to create a fragrant, balanced sauce. Only some of the oil is used to make the sauce; save the rest for drizzling into grain salads, stirring into soups, or brushing onto roasted vegetables. MAKES 1 CUP

- 1½ tablespoons neutral oil
- 1 tablespoon madras curry powder
- ¾ cup (189 g) sour cream
- ¼ cup (50 g) mayonnaise
- 2 teaspoons fresh lemon juice
- Kosher salt and freshly ground black pepper

In a small saucepan over low heat, combine the oil and curry powder. When the mixture starts to bubble and become fragrant, remove it from the heat and immediately pour it into a heatproof bowl. Let cool to room temperature.

In another small bowl, stir together the sour cream, mayonnaise, and lemon juice. Add 2 teaspoons of the cooled curry oil, saving the rest for other purposes. Season with salt and pepper. The curry cream can be made in advance and stored in an airtight container in the refrigerator for up to 5 days.

VARIATION

Lemon Cream

Bright and edgy, this lemon cream swaps curry oil for extra lemon juice and zest, making it a refreshing accompaniment to fish.

Omit the oil and curry powder and add 1 tablespoon more lemon juice plus the finely grated zest of 2 lemons to the sour cream mixture.

SPREADS & DIPS

3-Lentil Hummus, page 66
Seedy Crispbread, page 225
Roasted Carrot Hummus, page 71
sted Parsnip Spread, page 69

3-Lentil Hummus

You might find it unusual that hummus, a typically Middle Eastern food, has been included here, but the reason is simple: For years, vegetarian spreads have been part of the Scandinavian kitchen, and even more so now with the region's tremendous movement toward a plant-based diet. Hummus has been "adopted" into the cuisine as a healthy, protein-rich food that has as many variations as there are ways to serve it. In San Francisco, one of my favorite places to shop is Rainbow Grocery, a co-op with a bulk section that feels almost otherworldly. Grains, spices, pastas, teas, even a bulk kimchi section—they have almost everything, including just the right amount of French (du Puy) lentils, red lentils, and green lentils for this hummus.

This version—made without chickpeas—is earthy, creamy, and lightly spiced with cumin, and is perfect as a dip or slathered onto a veggie sandwich. If speckled, green-bluish-grayish French lentils prove hard to find, just double up on the more common, generic green lentils and call it 2-lentil hummus—it's still lovely and satisfying. **MAKES 2½ CUPS**

⅓ cup (65 g) French (du Puy) lentils

½ cup (100 g) green lentils

2 tablespoons red lentils

2 tablespoons extra-virgin olive oil, plus more for garnish

1 small garlic clove, minced

1 tablespoon finely chopped fresh flat-leaf parsley, plus a few leaves for garnish

½ teaspoon ground cumin

3 tablespoons fresh lemon juice, plus more as needed

⅓ cup (87 g) tahini

Kosher salt and freshly ground black pepper

Place the French and green lentils in a medium saucepan and add water to cover by 1 inch (2.5 cm). Bring to a boil over high heat, then decrease the heat to low and simmer, uncovered and stirring occasionally, for 15 minutes. Add the red lentils and additional water to cover. Increase the heat to high, bring to a boil, then decrease the heat to low and continue to simmer, stirring occasionally, until the lentils are tender but not mushy, 18 to 20 minutes longer. Drain the lentils in a fine-mesh sieve. Return them to the saucepan and set them aside to cool slightly.

While the lentils cool, in a small sauté pan over medium-low heat, warm the olive oil. Add the garlic and cook, swirling the pan for even cooking, until fragrant and golden but not browned, about 20 seconds. Remove the pan from the heat and stir in the parsley.

Put the lentils in a food processor and add the garlic-parsley oil, cumin, lemon juice, tahini, 1 teaspoon salt, and a few grinds of pepper. Process until smooth, stopping to scrape down the bowl once and adding water 1 tablespoon at a time to reach the consistency you desire. Adjust the consistency by adding more lemon juice or water until it is spoonable but not pasty. Season with more salt and pepper if needed.

To serve, smear onto a shallow bowl and garnish with a drizzle of olive oil and a few parsley leaves. The hummus can be refrigerated in an airtight container for up to 5 days.

Beet Hummus

Beet hummus is a bit of a show-off—unapologetically pink and impossible to ignore. When it's on the menu at Kantine, heads turn as smears of it on small plates are carried through the dining room. The beets bring an earthy sweetness that rounds out the nutty tahini and bright lemon. I love it spread thick on rye crispbread with a tangle of fresh sprouts or as a dip for crunchy vegetables. A spoonful on the side of a salad is an easy way to add both color and protein. **MAKES 3 CUPS**

1 cup (200 g) dried chickpeas, soaked overnight at room temperature (see Note)

8 ounces (224 g) red beets, trimmed (about 3 medium beets)

2 teaspoons kosher salt, plus more for cooking beets

¼ cup (65 g) tahini

1 tablespoon fresh lemon juice, plus more as needed

1 teaspoon ground cumin

3 tablespoons neutral oil

Freshly ground black pepper

Extra-virgin olive oil, for garnish

Sesame seeds, for garnish

Drain the chickpeas and transfer them to a medium saucepan. Add water to cover by 2 inches (5 cm) and bring to a boil over medium-high heat. Decrease the heat and simmer, until the chickpeas are soft without falling apart, 45 to 60 minutes, adding a bit more water if necessary to keep them covered. Skim and discard any foam that collects on the surface. Set aside.

Meanwhile, prepare the beets. Place the beets in a medium pot and add cold water to cover by about 1 inch (2.5 cm). Add a few pinches of salt and bring to a boil over high heat. Decrease the temperature to low and simmer for 20 to 40 minutes, depending on the size of the beets. Test for doneness with a fork. They should be tender in the middle like boiled potatoes. As they finish cooking, you may see their skins slipping off. Drain them in a colander and rinse under cold water, removing any remaining skin. Pat dry. With a chef's knife, cut the beets into 1-inch (2.5 cm) cubes.

Drain the cooked chickpeas, reserving 2 cups (480 g) of the cooking liquid. Measure out 1¾ cups (300 g) of chickpeas and 1 cup (200 g) cubed beets. You will likely have a smidge more than necessary of each. Use the surplus in other recipes.

Put roughly half the chickpeas and the beets in a food processor. Add half of the tahini, half of the lemon juice, half of the cumin, 2 teaspoons salt, and 1½ tablespoons of the neutral oil. Process until smooth, stopping to scrape down the bowl a few times. Add a splash of cooking liquid to keep things moving. Once you have a homogeneous puree, transfer the hummus to a medium bowl and repeat with the remaining chickpeas, beets, tahini, lemon juice, and cumin, and the remaining 1½ tablespoons neutral oil. Add the rest of the hummus to the same bowl, stir to combine, and season with salt and pepper. Adjust the consistency with lemon juice or cooking liquid until it is spoonable without being pasty.

Serve in a shallow bowl, garnished with a drizzle of olive oil and a sprinkle of sesame seeds. The hummus can be kept in an airtight container in the refrigerator for 5 days.

Note

The hummus is made with 1¾ cups (300 g) cooked chickpeas. If you'd like to use canned chickpeas instead, drain and rinse the chickpeas, then measure out 1¾ cups (300 g) and use water as the liquid for pureeing.

Kale Tahini Spread

Kale's status as a super food doesn't mean that it's something we always consume enough of, but this dark green spread makes eating your greens a no-brainer. The tahini smooths out the kale's grassy bite, while lemon and garlic keep things bright. I love it smeared on good bread, as part of a snack board, or tucked alongside roasted meats. There's no kale waste here—the stems are part of what helps bulk this spread up. Feel free to substitute lacinato or purple kale for the curly green kale, if that's what you have. **MAKES 2 CUPS**

- 1 bunch of curly green kale (8¾ ounces / 252 g)
- ¼ cup (55 g) extra-virgin olive oil, plus more for garnish
- 1 garlic clove, minced
- 3 tablespoons tahini
- Zest of 1 lemon
- 1 tablespoon fresh lemon juice
- Kosher salt and freshly ground black pepper

Bring a large pot of salted water to a boil over high heat. Fill a large bowl with ice water. Add the kale to the boiling water and cook, stirring, until the stems are tender, about 5 minutes. Transfer the kale to the ice bath and let it stand for 3 to 4 minutes.

In a small skillet over medium heat, warm the olive oil. Add the garlic and cook, stirring, until fragrant and golden in color, about 3 minutes. Set the garlic oil aside to cool.

Remove the kale from the ice bath and squeeze out any excess water. Coarsely chop the kale and transfer it to a food processor along with the garlic oil, tahini, lemon zest and juice, and ¾ teaspoon salt. Process the mixture, stopping to scrape down the bowl once, until similar in consistency to hummus (it's okay if it's a bit chunky). Feel free to add a splash of water, if necessary, to keep things moving in the processor.

Transfer the spread to a medium bowl and stir thoroughly to ensure it's evenly combined. Season with salt and pepper. Serve, garnished with a drizzle of olive oil. The spread tastes best when it's just been made, but it can be kept in an airtight container (with just enough olive oil to cover the surface) in the refrigerator for 1 to 2 days.

Roasted Parsnip Spread

Parsnips are common in Scandinavia. They thrive in cold climates and were once a staple crop in northern Europe before potatoes took over from about the sixteenth century. Sweeter and more complex than carrots, they take well to roasting, which brings out their natural nuttiness. In this spread, they are blended with walnuts, dill, and a good glug of olive oil for something creamy and earthy with a hint of sweetness. It's great smeared on toasted rye bread, scooped up with crackers, or spooned onto a plate next to roasted chicken. A little old-world, a little new, and completely worth making. **MAKES 2 CUPS**

- 12 ounces (336 g) parsnips, scrubbed and cut into 1-inch (2.5 cm) chunks (3 or 4 medium parsnips)
- 1 bunch of dill, plus a few sprigs for garnish
- Kosher salt and freshly ground black pepper
- ⅓ cup (73 g) extra-virgin olive oil, plus more for garnish
- 2 garlic cloves, minced
- 2 tablespoons fresh lemon juice, plus more as needed
- ½ cup (43 g) walnut pieces
- Pinch of crushed red pepper flakes

Preheat the oven to 350°F (175°C).

Place the parsnips and dill in a 2-quart (2L) baking dish. Season with salt and pepper and add enough water to come halfway up the parsnips. Cover with a lid or aluminum foil and bake until very soft and mashable (like a baked potato), 45 to 60 minutes.

Drain, reserving any remaining cooking liquid. Transfer the parsnips and dill to a food processor.

In a small skillet over medium heat, warm the olive oil. Add the garlic and cook, stirring, until fragrant and golden in color, about 3 minutes. Remove from the heat and pour the garlic oil over the parsnips and dill in the food processor, then add the lemon juice and walnuts.

Process the mixture, stopping to scrape down the bowl a few times and adding enough reserved cooking liquid to get everything moving; add water as needed until the mixture is quite smooth (you may need up to 1½ cups / 360 g). The consistency should be similar to hummus: spoonable but not thick or pasty.

Transfer the spread to a medium bowl and stir thoroughly to ensure it's evenly combined. Season with salt, red pepper flakes, and, if you like, add a touch more lemon juice.

Serve in a shallow bowl, garnished with a drizzle of olive oil and a few dill sprigs. The spread can be kept in an airtight container in the refrigerator for 5 days.

Tinned Smoked Sardine Spread

Whenever I'm scrounging in the kitchen for something quick to eat, I'm always happy to come across my stack of tinned fish. Tinned fish is something I keep on hand for its long shelf life and deep, umami flavor; it's also a quick and easy source of protein and healthy fats. Here, smoked sardines are pulsed into a smooth, spreadable dip that can be served as an appetizer or as part of a "seacuterie" snack board with rye bread, sliced radishes, cucumber, and chives. If you don't like or have smoked sardines, smoked mackerel or kippers work just as well for a slightly different take. **MAKES ¾ CUP**

5¼ ounces (150 g) boneless, skinless wild smoked sardine fillets (I'm particularly fond of the brands Fishwife and Bar Harbor)

2 tablespoons plain skyr or Greek yogurt

2 teaspoons fresh lemon juice

½ teaspoon Dijon mustard

Kosher salt and freshly ground black pepper

FOR SERVING

Thinly sliced rye bread or rye crackers

1 small bunch of radishes, trimmed and thinly sliced

1 small cucumber, thinly sliced

1 bunch of chives, chopped

Place the sardines in an immersion blender container. Add the yogurt, lemon juice, and mustard, and season with a pinch of salt and a little pepper. Using an immersion blender, blend the mixture, stopping briefly to scrape down the container once, until the consistency is smooth and creamy. If it is too thick, add water 1 teaspoon at a time to achieve the texture you desire. (If you don't have an immersion blender, you can use a bowl with a whisk or a food processor.)

Spread the dip into a serving dish and chill for at least 30 minutes. Serve spread with sliced rye bread, radish, cucumber, and lots of chives.

Roasted Carrot Hummus

My partner is Danish, and when people ask him what foods he misses most from Scandinavia, he usually says carrots! Carrots over there have a grassy sweetness that makes them particularly delightful to eat raw, but recently we've found carrots at the farmers' market that have squelched his yearning. Roasting the carrots as disks brings out their natural sweetness, which makes a tasty contrast to the lemon and spices. **MAKES 3 CUPS**

¾ cup (150 g) dried chickpeas, soaked overnight at room temperature (see Note)

1 pound (454 g) carrots, scrubbed and cut into ¼-inch (6 mm) disks

½ cup (110 g) plus 2 tablespoons neutral oil

3 teaspoons kosher salt, plus more for seasoning the carrots and as needed

Freshly ground black pepper

¼ cup (65 g) tahini

2 tablespoons fresh lemon juice, plus more as needed

2 teaspoons ground coriander

2 teaspoons ground cumin

2 teaspoons sumac, plus more for garnish

2 teaspoons chili powder

Extra-virgin olive oil, for garnish

Sesame seeds, for garnish

Drain the chickpeas and transfer them to a medium saucepan. Add water to cover by 2 inches (5 cm) and bring to a boil over medium-high heat. Decrease the heat and simmer until the chickpeas are soft without falling apart, 45 to 60 minutes, adding a bit more water if necessary to keep them covered. Skim and discard any foam that collects on the surface. Set aside.

Meanwhile, prepare the carrots. Preheat the oven to 350°F (175°C). Line a 13 by 18-inch (33 by 46 cm) baking tray with parchment paper.

In a medium bowl, toss the carrots with 2 tablespoons of the neutral oil, season with a bit of salt and pepper, then spread them out evenly on the prepared baking tray. Bake, rotating the tray halfway through, until soft and lightly browned, 30 to 45 minutes.

Drain the chickpeas, reserving 2 cups (480 g) of the cooking liquid. Measure out 1¾ cups (300 g) chickpeas and 1⅓ cups (225 g) roasted carrots. You will likely have a smidge more than necessary of each. Use the surplus in other recipes.

Put roughly half the chickpeas and the roasted carrots in a food processor. Add half of the tahini, half of the lemon juice, and half of the spices along with 2 teaspoons of the salt and ¼ cup (55 g) of the neutral oil and process until smooth, stopping to scrape down the bowl a few times. Add a splash of cooking liquid to keep things moving. I prefer to keep the hummus a tad chunky, but if you like a smooth hummus, process it longer and add a bit more liquid, if needed.

Transfer the hummus to a medium bowl and repeat with the remaining chickpeas, carrots, tahini, lemon juice, spices, 1 teaspoon salt, and ¼ cup neutral oil. Add the rest of the hummus to the same bowl, stir to combine, and season with salt and pepper. Adjust the consistency with lemon juice or cooking liquid until the hummus is spoonable without being pasty.

Serve in a shallow bowl, garnished with a drizzle of olive oil and a sprinkle of sesame seeds and sumac. The hummus can be kept in an airtight container in the refrigerator for 5 days.

Note

The hummus is made with 1¾ cups (300 g) cooked chickpeas. If you'd like to use canned chickpeas instead, drain and rinse the chickpeas, then measure out 1¾ cups (300 g) and use water as the liquid for pureeing.

BOWL ME OVER

On weekdays in Scandinavia, breakfast is normally simple and quick. A cup of coffee or tea, a few slices of buttered bread topped with meat or cheese, or a bowl of yogurt—that's it. And for those who prefer going to the local bakery, a BMO (*bolle med ost,* or buttered bun with sliced cheese) on the way to work is a perfect grab-and-go item.

And then there are the weekends. When I lived in Copenhagen, my family and I would often take advantage of the leisurely mornings and make porridge for breakfast at least once during the weekend.

When I was growing up in Ohio, porridge was synonymous with sugary instant oatmeal from a pouch. For some others I know, the word *porridge* conjures images of thick, pasty gruel that seems more suited to hanging wallpaper than for eating. But it doesn't have to be that way. In my opinion, porridge just doesn't get the credit it deserves. When my partner and I became parents, we began making simple porridges using wholesome grains and toppings, which felt perfectly fitting as our children's first foods. As our kids grew, so did our fondness for porridge, most often as a family. Eventually it became a set weekend tradition with a big, steaming pot for everyone to enjoy.

Around 2010, a porridge renaissance began stirring in Scandinavia, and luckily, I was living there at the time. Suddenly, new ingredients and fresh ideas were finding their way into bowls across the region. I remember the buzz around the opening of the first "porridge bar," called Grød, in Copenhagen, and, just like that, people were standing in long lines just to get their hands on a bowl of it! But despite its popularity, it wasn't until I became head chef at a preschool for 240 hungry kids (and their teachers) that my passion for porridge was ignited.

We'd serve porridge—sometimes savory, sometimes sweet—for lunch once a week. Not only was it something the kids loved, but it was economical, easy to make in large batches, and endlessly versatile. We'd send big bowls of hot porridge to each classroom along with smaller bowls of toppings. Under the watchful eye of a teacher, the kids would serve themselves. Most often, the bowls came back completely empty.

My porridge game improved with time, so much so that years later, when I competed in Copenhagen's Porridge Championship (I kid you not), I finished second. And then, a few years later, after my family and I had moved to San Francisco, I started selling porridge bowls (and sprouted rye bread) at the Ferry Plaza farmers' market and hosted porridge pop-ups in the Mission, as a way to introduce Americans to one of my most beloved foods. That's how porridge became something more to me—a dish I played around with, championed, and, ultimately, shared with a whole new audience.

This may be the shortest chapter in the book but possibly the one with the most potential. Once you start making these bowls, you might feel more inclined to riff on a porridge yourself—tweaking and improvising to create something uniquely yours. It's bound to change your mind completely about what porridge can be.

Sweet 3-Grain Porridge

with Pear, Date-Walnut Butter, and Crispy Buckwheat

This porridge is a mix of buckwheat and two different kinds of oats: groats and flakes. If you're wondering, groats (sometimes referred to as "berries") are whole grains (see more on page 35) that have had the inedible hull removed. Grains in this form are extremely nutritious and give porridge such a satisfying chew. If it's not pear season, use any other ripe fruit you have on hand; this base works any time of year with all kinds of toppings (see Porridge Topping Sets, page 79, for more ideas).

Often, I'll make the porridge base at the beginning of the week, eat one portion, and then refrigerate the rest to have breakfast sorted for a few days. I reheat the base with a splash of milk or water, either in the microwave or a saucepan. Easy peasy. And if you ever have leftover sweet porridge, I urge you to make Leftover Porridge Cakes with Cardamom, Skyr, and Crushed Red Berries (page 89). **MAKES 4 SERVINGS**

DATE-WALNUT BUTTER

- 5 ounces (140 g) dates (preferably Medjool), pitted
- 1 cup (240 g) water
- ½ cup (43 g) walnuts
- ½ teaspoon vanilla extract
- Pinch of kosher salt

CRISPY BUCKWHEAT

- ½ cup (90 g) buckwheat groats
- 1 teaspoon neutral oil, plus more for greasing
- 2 teaspoons sugar
- ½ teaspoon ground cinnamon
- Pinch of kosher salt

PORRIDGE BASE

- 1 cup (190 g) oat groats
- 1 cup (105 g) old-fashioned rolled oats
- Pinch of kosher salt
- 1 tablespoon unsalted butter
- 1 tablespoon runny honey
- 2 ripe but firm pears (preferably d'Anjou or Bosc), cut in quarters, then into ¼-inch (6 mm) slices

Make the date-walnut butter. In a small saucepan, combine the dates, water, walnuts, vanilla, and salt. Cover the pan and bring to a boil over high heat. Decrease the heat to low and simmer gently until the dates are very soft, about 8 minutes. Pour ½ cup (120 g) of the cooking liquid into a small bowl and keep it close by—you'll use it to adjust the consistency of the butter. Pour the rest of the contents from the pan into a blender. Blend until completely smooth, adding as much of the reserved liquid as necessary to get things moving around well. The ideal consistency should be similar to that of Greek yogurt. Transfer to a bowl and set aside until the porridge is ready or refrigerate in an airtight container for up to 4 days before serving.

Make the crispy buckwheat. Put the buckwheat groats in a small saucepan and add water to cover by about 1 inch (2.5 cm). Bring to a boil over high heat and boil for 3 minutes. Drain, discarding the cooking water, then rinse the buckwheat briefly with cold water. Spread out on a baking tray to cool. When cool, set aside ¼ cup (38 g) for your porridge base.

Preheat the oven to 350°F (175°C). Lightly oil a 13 by 18-inch (33 by 46 cm) baking tray.

In a small bowl, stir together the remaining cooked buckwheat with the 1 teaspoon oil, the sugar, cinnamon, and salt. Spread out on the prepared tray and bake, rotating the tray and giving it a stir halfway through, until the buckwheat is dry, 30 minutes. (The buckwheat gets crispier as it cools, so don't look for that as a sign of doneness.) Let cool completely before transferring to an airtight container. The crispy buckwheat can be made in advance and stored at room temperature for at least 1 week.

CONTINUED

Sweet 3-Grain Porridge with Pear, Date-Walnut Butter, and Crispy Buckwheat, CONTINUED

Make the porridge. Put the oat groats in a medium saucepan and add water to cover by about 2 inches (5 cm). Bring to a boil over medium-high heat, then decrease the heat to medium and simmer gently for 15 minutes. Pour in the oats and the reserved parboiled buckwheat. Add a touch more water, if necessary, to keep the porridge loose and prevent scorching on the bottom of your pan. Decrease the heat to low and simmer for 15 minutes more. Check for doneness by ensuring that the grains are soft and the oat groats are tender in the center but still have a chewy texture.

(If you aren't going to be serving all the porridge at once, prepare it to this point and spread out the amount to be stored on a baking tray to cool quickly. Once cool, store in an airtight container in the refrigerator for up to 4 days and reheat as needed.)

To finish the porridge, stir in the salt, butter, and honey and give it a final taste. The aim is to make a porridge that is not overly sweet, has a good balance of salt (without tasting salty), and is ever so comforting to eat, even without the toppings.

Divide the porridge among four bowls. Arrange the pear slices on top, spoon the date-walnut butter off to one side, and sprinkle the crispy buckwheat on top. Serve immediately.

porridge bases 101

I am a PPP—a Passionate Porridge Person—and I'm hoping that the recipes in this chapter will turn you into one, too. Honestly, I could have written an entire book about porridge, but so much of the fun is in exploring the subject on your own, because there are endless ways to make stellar porridges. Truly outstanding porridges can be made with minimal effort and just a handful of ingredients.

Most of the time, when I'm making porridge, I lean toward a medley of two or more grains as my base: usually one whole grain, like quinoa, rye berries, or buckwheat groats, plus a grain flake, like old-fashioned rolled oats or wheat or barley flakes. Sometimes I'll add in a third ingredient, which could be a cut grain (as in the rye grits in Savory 3-Grain Porridge with Kale, Mushrooms, and Farmers Cheese, page 81), but I also often incorporate legumes such as beans and lentils into my base. (They need to be cooked separately in advance of mixing with the base.) The ratio of whole grain to flake is yours to play with, depending on the grain and your preference. I find that whole grains add chewiness and bulk, while flakes bring soft, velvety creaminess.

Usually, I start a batch of porridge by parboiling the grain (or grains) in water until tender. Cooking them in water keeps the base neutral, and if I'm using a grain mix, I cook them separately, since each has its own cooking time. Once cooked, I spread them out onto a baking tray to cool, then mix them together—this is the porridge base. It can be prepared in advance and stored in an airtight container in the refrigerator for up to 4 days. To serve the porridge, the grains are reheated with liquid—preferably a flavorful one, like stock, whey, or milk. Butter, olive oil, lemon zest, and ground spices are delightful additions to stir in near the end, and salt is absolutely essential to making porridge taste right. I often think of what a former chef I worked for used to say: "Add enough salt, but not so much that the food actually tastes salty," and that includes sweet preparations, too. The right amount of salt will make your porridge pop.

porridge topping sets

A tasty porridge base goes a long way, but toppings can really bring it over the finish line. The right set of toppings boosts flavor, texture, and appearance.

Here are a few of my favorite combinations, both savory and sweet:

savory

- roasted asparagus, peas, silken leeks (from Warm Potato Salad with Silken Leeks and Celery Seed Vinaigrette, page 112)
- avocado chunks, crispy bacon bits, chopped kale, chili crisp
- flakes of smoked trout, Perfect Poached Egg (page 85)
- roasted winter squash, browned breakfast sausage meat, Farmers Cheese (page 82)
- crispy tofu, sliced scallions, garlicky sautéed spinach

sweet

- fresh figs, toasted hazelnuts, lemon zest, brown butter
- Whole Roasted Apple Compote (page 92), skyr, almond butter, date syrup
- Shaken Red Currants (page 196), fresh raspberries, mint-tarragon sugar (made in a mortar), a splash of heavy cream
- oven-roasted rhubarb (from Rhubarb Cake with Custard Sauce, page 249), spoonfuls of your favorite granola, a sprinkle of freshly ground cardamom

Savory 3-Grain Porridge

with Kale, Mushrooms, and Farmers Cheese

This porridge has been a favorite of mine since long before we opened Kantine. When the line cooks see me head toward the stovetop with a bowl in hand, they know that I'm looking to raid the porridge pot. By the way, don't let anyone tell you that porridge can be eaten only for breakfast. Personally, I have it for lunch several times a week! If you prefer to buy farmers cheese, you'll be missing whey to finish the porridge with—in that case, use half water, half buttermilk instead. As with any porridge, you should consider topping it with a Perfect Poached Egg (page 85). **MAKES 4 SERVINGS**

- ⅔ cup (113 g) cracked rye
- ½ cup (90 g) quinoa
- 3 cups (720 g) water
- ½ cup (85 g) wheat berries
- ¼ cup (55 g) extra-virgin olive oil
- 3 cups (720 g) whey from Farmers Cheese (recipe follows), plus more as needed
- 1 bunch of lacinato or curly green kale (9 ounces / 252 g), ribs removed and leaves chopped into bite-size pieces
- Kosher salt and freshly ground black pepper
- 4 ounces (112 g) cremini mushrooms, quartered
- 4 ounces (112 g) mixed mushrooms, like shiitake (stems removed), maitake, and oyster, cut into bite-size pieces
- ½ cup (140 g) Farmers Cheese (recipe follows)
- Ground turmeric, for garnish
- ¼ cup (37 g) toasted sunflower seeds (see Toasting Nuts and Seeds, page 42)

In a medium saucepan, combine the cracked rye, quinoa, and water. Put the wheat berries in a separate small saucepan and add water to cover by 1 inch (2.5 cm; there's no need to measure the water here, as the berries are drained afterward). Bring each pan to a boil. Decrease the heat to low and cook, uncovered, until the grains are cooked through, about 25 minutes for the rye and quinoa and 30 to 35 minutes for the wheat berries. Add a smidge more water, as needed, to prevent scorching. Check for doneness by ensuring that the rye and quinoa are soft and the wheat berries are tender in the center but still have a chewy texture.

When the wheat berries are done, drain the excess water and add them to the saucepan with the rye and quinoa. This unseasoned trio of grains is your porridge base. If you aren't going to be serving all the porridge at once, prepare it to this point, spreading out the amount to be stored on a baking tray to cool quickly. Once cool, store in an airtight container in the refrigerator for up to 4 days and reheat as needed.

To finish preparing all the porridge at once, add 2 tablespoons of the olive oil and the whey to the pot with the porridge base. Bring the porridge to a simmer over medium heat, stirring occasionally. Once hot, stir in the kale and season with salt and pepper. Decrease the heat to low while you prepare the mushrooms.

In a medium skillet over medium heat, warm the remaining 2 tablespoons olive oil. Add the cremini mushrooms and cook, stirring occasionally, until they begin to soften and release their liquid, 3 to 4 minutes. Add the mixed mushrooms to the same pan, sprinkle with salt and pepper, and continue to cook, stirring occasionally, until tender and juicy, 4 to 5 more minutes. Pour the mushrooms into a bowl and set aside while you finish the porridge.

CONTINUED

Savory 3-Grain Porridge with Kale, Mushrooms, and Farmers Cheese, CONTINUED

The final porridge consistency you're looking for falls somewhere between risotto and rice soup. It should be bowlable but not stiff, so adjust the consistency of yours with a tad more water or whey, and if it's too watery, cook your porridge a little longer to tighten it up.

When it's ready, give it one last taste for seasoning, then divide the porridge among four shallow bowls. Spoon the sautéed mushrooms and farmers cheese over the top of each bowl of porridge, allowing them to fall in small bits across the entire surface. (I love when there's a bit of topping in each spoonful.) Garnish each bowl with a sprinkle of turmeric and toasted sunflower seeds. Serve immediately.

Farmers Cheese

This farmers cheese has a consistency similar to ricotta and is made from just three ingredients. Through experience, I've found that the slower the mixture is brought to temperature, the creamier the final cheese will be. Once it's removed from the heat, the curds need time to firm up in their liquidy whey, preferably overnight. This not only makes straining easier but also results in a higher yield.

And don't discard the whey! You'll need some to make Savory 3-Grain Porridge with Kale, Mushrooms, and Farmers Cheese (page 81), and it can also be used in bread or pizza doughs or added to soup or even smoothies. **MAKES 2 CUPS**

- 4 cups (960 g) buttermilk
- ¾ cup (180 g) heavy cream
- 1 teaspoon kosher salt

In a medium heavy-bottomed saucepan over medium-low heat, combine the buttermilk, cream, and salt. You'll notice after a few minutes that the edges will begin to coagulate. Don't stir the cheese at any point, but instead rotate the pot a few quarter-turns while heating to even out any hot spots. Your target temperature is 190°F (90°C), so have an instant-read thermometer handy and start checking every 5 minutes or so until the temperature has been reached, about 15 minutes total.

Remove the pot from the heat and cool on the stovetop for at least 1 hour, up to 4 hours, or overnight in the refrigerator. Gently pour the contents of the pot over a fine-mesh sieve set over a large bowl to catch the whey. Gently press on the cheese with the back of a spoon to release a bit more whey. Transfer the cheese and whey to two separate airtight containers. The cheese can be stored in an airtight container in the refrigerator for 5 days.

perfect poached eggs

So many recipes in this book would benefit from a poached egg on top, Barley Porridge with Spinach and Smoked Salmon (page 86) and Kale and Einkorn Salad with Mirabelles and Walnut Vinaigrette (page 119) to name a couple. But poached eggs can feel like such a daunting kitchen task—my first attempt in high school home ec resulted in something closer to egg drop soup. With this method, inspired by America's Test Kitchen, it's a no-brainer. What could be easier than pouring the eggs in water and not touching them for 5 minutes? Grade AA eggs work best since their firm whites hold their shape better. It's important that you come as close to the correct pan size as possible so that the cooking times and technique remain unchanged. MAKES 1 TO 8 EGGS

1 to 8 eggs (Grade AA if possible)

2 tablespoons white vinegar

2 teaspoons kosher salt, plus more for seasoning

Freshly ground black pepper

Fill a 3-quart (3L) straight-sided sauté pan with water, leaving about 1 inch (2.5 cm) of space to the rim. Add the vinegar and salt and cover the pan. Bring to a boil over high heat.

Meanwhile, prepare your eggs. Crack 1 to 2 eggs into shallow cups (like a wide-mouthed teacup) or ramekin. You'll be able to cook 8 eggs at once if you use four cups with 2 eggs in each. (If a yolk breaks, save the egg for another recipe and redo.)

Once the water is boiling, slide the pan off the heat and turn off the burner. Take the lid off, swiftly lower the cup bottoms into the water, then tip the rim so the eggs can flow into the hot water. Replace the lid and let the eggs stand in the water for 4½ to 5 minutes (see Note). Line a plate with a few pieces of paper towel and, when the timer rings, carefully transfer the eggs one at a time with a slotted spoon to the plate to absorb the excess water. Season with salt and pepper and carefully move the egg to your bread, salad, or porridge.

Note

The 4½- to 5-minute cooking time is for up to 8 eggs. For 9 or more eggs, increase the cooking time to about 7 minutes.

Barley Porridge

with Spinach and Smoked Salmon

I am a savory morning person until the first craving for *fika* (see page 250) hits around 10 a.m. But this porridge is just as good any time of day, with its mix of creamy barley, wilted spinach, and smoky salmon. If you aren't able to smoke your own salmon, store-bought hot-smoked salmon or trout works as a quick fix. To boost the nutrition, you can swap in hulled barley for pearled, but the cooking time will need to increase to about 50 minutes. And if you really want to take it over the top, add a Perfect Poached Egg (page 85)—highly recommended. **MAKES 4 SERVINGS**

- 1½ cups (300 g) pearled barley
- 1 tablespoon neutral oil
- 1 tablespoon unsalted butter
- 1 small shallot, thinly sliced
- Kosher salt and freshly ground black pepper
- 4 cups (960 g) water
- 2 cups (40 g) loosely packed baby spinach
- 2 tablespoons chopped fresh chives
- 2 tablespoons chopped fresh dill, plus a few sprigs for garnish
- 1 teaspoon fresh lemon juice
- 8 ounces (224 g) Oven-Smoked Salmon (page 200), flaked into chunks
- ½ lemon, for squeezing, as needed
- Extra-virgin olive oil, for garnish

In a spice grinder or blender, grind ½ cup of the barley into a very coarse flour. Set aside.

In a medium saucepan over medium heat, heat the oil and butter until the butter melts. Add the shallot to the pan and cook, stirring, until soft, about 1 minute. Add the remaining 1 cup barley and a pinch of salt and cook, stirring constantly, until there are some flecks of color on the grains and the barley smells toasted, 2 minutes. Add the pulverized barley and the water to the pan. Bring to a boil over medium-high heat, then decrease the heat to low, cover, and simmer until the barley is very tender and creamy, about 20 minutes. Remove from the heat and set aside, covered, for 5 to 10 minutes.

The porridge base can be prepared in advance and stored in an airtight container in the refrigerator for 3 days. To reheat, add a splash of water and proceed with the recipe.

Just before serving, stir in the spinach, chives, chopped dill, and lemon juice and simmer just until the spinach wilts, about 30 seconds. Season with salt and pepper.

Divide the porridge among four bowls. Dot each portion with pieces of salmon, then garnish with dill sprigs. Squeeze the ½ lemon and drizzle a little olive oil over each bowl. Serve immediately.

Leftover Porridge Cakes

with Cardamom, Skyr, and Crushed Red Berries

A twist on traditional Danish *klatkage,* pancakes made from leftover rice porridge around the holidays, these porridge cakes make great use of leftover sweet porridge at any time of the year. They are easy to throw together and cook up beautifully, whether you're using fresh or frozen berries. Skyr, the silky Icelandic yogurt, adds a boost of protein. And if you want even-size cakes without a hassle, a spring-loaded scoop makes getting them into the pan a piece of cake (no pun intended). **MAKES 18 CAKES**

CRUSHED RED BERRIES

1 cup (123 g) fresh raspberries

⅓ cup (45 g) hulled and sliced fresh strawberries

¼ cup (50 g) sugar

1 tablespoon fresh lemon juice

CAKES

1⅓ cups (346 g) cooked and cooled porridge

2 eggs, separated

2 tablespoons all-purpose flour, plus more as needed

1 tablespoon sugar

1 teaspoon vanilla extract

½ teaspoon ground cardamom, plus more as needed

Finely grated zest of ½ lemon

Kosher salt

About ¼ cup (55 g) neutral oil

1 tablespoon cold unsalted butter, cut into small pieces

1½ cups (390 g) plain skyr or Greek yogurt

Make the berries. In a small saucepan over low heat, combine the berries, sugar, and lemon juice. The goal is to heat the berries slowly and dissolve the sugar while keeping the mixture from bubbling or simmering. Cook until the berries are soft and have begun to break down, about 15 minutes (longer if using frozen berries). Transfer the mixture to a small bowl and mash lightly with a fork, still keeping a bit of chunkiness. Let cool to room temperature. If not using immediately, transfer to an airtight container and refrigerate for up to 1 week.

Make the cakes. In a large bowl, combine the leftover porridge, egg yolks, 2 tablespoons flour, the sugar, vanilla, cardamom, lemon zest, and a pinch of salt. Stir until a thick, cohesive batter forms.

In the bowl of a stand mixer fitted with the whisk attachment or in a medium bowl with a whisk, whip the egg whites with a pinch of salt on medium speed until soft peaks form. Using a rubber spatula, fold half of the egg whites into the porridge mixture and, once incorporated, repeat with the remaining egg whites.

Heat a medium skillet over medium heat. Add a small amount of oil in a corner of the pan and fry a test cake: Spoon a tablespoon of batter into the pan and decrease the heat to low. Fry until golden brown and crisp, turning once, 6 to 8 minutes. Taste the cake and adjust the batter as necessary by gently stirring in 1 to 2 more tablespoons of flour (if it seems too wet), a splash of milk (if it seems too stiff), or even a pinch more cardamom or salt.

Working in batches, add 1 tablespoon of oil to the pan over medium heat. Drop heaping tablespoons of the batter onto the pan. Drop small pieces of butter into the skillet every so often while the cakes cook. Cook until golden brown and crisp, turning once, 6 to 8 minutes. Transfer the cooked cakes to a plate to keep warm and repeat with the remaining batter. Serve hot, accompanied by the skyr and crushed berries.

Honey Toasted Sesame Oats

with Filmjölk and Watermelon

These honey toasted oats are a longtime favorite. Years ago, I moved from Copenhagen to Cleveland for a short while, and while there I began dabbling in food writing. When I pitched a granola story to the local paper, they gave me the assignment and I created this recipe for a skillet granola (no oven needed) that reminded me of a favorite I used to enjoy in Denmark. Sesame fans, this is right up your alley. Together with a homemade yogurt called *filmjölk* and juicy watermelon, it's a mix of flavors and textures I never get tired of.

Filmjölk, or *fil* for short, is a Swedish cultured dairy product rich in protein and probiotics. I used to buy it often at the store near our small summerhouse in Sweden. After we sold the house, I missed eating it for breakfast, but then I found a filmjölk culture starter online and began making my own. Unlike regular yogurt, which requires the milk to be heated before the culture is added, fil's fermentation starts simply at room temperature.

To make this recipe, you'll have to already have activated your culture and have filmjölk on hand. (Or if you prefer, you can substitute your favorite plain yogurt.) My experience with activation was that the first batch took almost 30 hours to make, but each batch since then has been considerably quicker, around 20 hours. And then to make the next batch, a single tablespoon of filmjölk gets stirred into milk and left at room temperature until thick—voilà, that's how easy it is. **MAKES 4 SERVINGS**

HONEY TOASTED SESAME OATS

- ¼ cup (56 g) unsalted butter
- ¼ cup (80 g) runny honey
- ¼ teaspoon kosher salt
- ½ cup (80 g) sesame seeds
- 1 cup (105 g) old-fashioned rolled oats
- 1 cup (104 g) quick oats
- ⅓ cup (40 g) raisins
- ¼ teaspoon ground cardamom

FOR SERVING

- 2 cups (504 g) filmjölk (or plain skyr or Greek yogurt)
- 3 cups (414 g) fresh watermelon in 1-inch (2.5 cm) chunks
- 2 tablespoons sprouted pumpkin seeds
- ¼ cup (45 g) sea buckthorn (optional)
- Your favorite floral runny honey (optional)

In a medium saucepan over medium heat, heat the butter, honey, and salt together until the butter has melted. Stir in the sesame seeds and decrease the heat to low. Stir constantly while the seeds cook, until golden. Stir in both kinds of oats and continue to stir until the oats have some touches of brown and are fragrant, 5 minutes. Remove the pan from the heat, quickly stir in the raisins and cardamom, and spread the mixture out onto a baking tray to cool. The oats can be stored in an airtight container at room temperature for up to 2 weeks.

To serve, put ½ cup (125 g) filmjölk into each of four cereal bowls. Divide the watermelon among the bowls and top each with ¼ cup of the toasted oats. Garnish each with pumpkin seeds and, if you like, sea buckthorn and drizzled of honey for added sweetness.

CONTINUED

VARIATION

Whole Roasted Apple Compote

For a winter version, swap whole roasted apples for the watermelon. Baking them whole means less waste, and a more concentrated flavor, turning them into a naturally sweet, spoonable compote. I tuck a few dates into the center of each apple to plump up in the apples' juices as they bake. Since I don't own an apple corer, I use a melon baller to core my apples and it works like a charm. Paired with the same filmjölk and skillet granola, this version feels extra cozy on cold mornings. **MAKES 2 CUPS**

3 large apples (preferably Braeburn or Fuji)

Kosher salt

9 to 12 dates (preferably Medjool), pitted

Preheat the oven to 400°F (200°C).

Core the apples and score the peel in 4 to 5 places from top to bottom (this will help with removing the skin later). Very lightly salt the inside of the apples. Stuff the core of each apple with 3 or 4 dates. Place the apples into a small oven-safe dish and bake, uncovered, until they have puffed up, maybe exuded a little juicy foam, and are soft to the touch, about 40 minutes. Remove from the oven and let cool.

Gently peel the apples with your fingers and discard the skin. Pour any liquid in the bottom of the baking dish into a bowl. With a chef's knife, chop the apple flesh and dates into smaller pieces, then transfer to the bowl with the cooking liquid. Stir to combine. Serve on top of the filmjölk with the honey toasted sesame oats.

Chocolate Muesli
with Orange and Cashews

Like overnight oats, this muesli softens as it sits, but it's ready in about an hour—just enough time for the chia seeds to plump up and the rolled oats to soften. Oat milk keeps it dairy-free, but any milk works just fine here. The word *muesli* usually refers to an unbaked granola that needs milk added, but here, the liquid is already mixed in. All that's left is for you to grab a spoon.

MAKES 5 CUPS

- 4 cups (960 g) oat milk
- 2 medium bananas
- 2 tablespoons quality cocoa powder
- Finely grated zest and juice of 1 orange
- 2 tablespoons runny honey or agave
- ½ teaspoon vanilla extract
- 2 cups (210 g) quick oats
- 1½ cups (157 g) old-fashioned rolled oats
- ¼ cup (45 g) cashew pieces, chopped
- 4 dates (preferably Medjool), pitted and finely chopped
- 2 tablespoons chia
- 1 teaspoon kosher salt
- 1 medium tart apple (preferably Braeburn), cored and shredded on the large holes of a box grater

In a blender, combine the oat milk, bananas, cocoa powder, orange zest and juice, honey, and vanilla. Blend on high speed to a frothy, homogeneous shake. In a medium bowl, stir together the two types of oats, the cashews, dates, chia, and salt. Pour the oat milk mixture over the oat mixture and stir to combine, then stir in the shredded apple. Cover and refrigerate for at least 20 minutes, allowing the chia seeds to soften. Enjoy right away or store in an airtight container in the refrigerator for 3 days.

Overnight Oats

with Hazelnut and Licorice Root

In Denmark, it's not uncommon to see people chewing on a gnarly strip of fresh licorice root, savoring its sweet, mellow flavor, which is much more approachable than that of black licorice candy. In the United States, the powdered form is easy to find online or in natural food stores, since consuming the root has loads of health benefits, from liver support to boosting immunity. If you have some powder to spare, try adding it to a chai spice blend or even a batch of chocolate chip cookies for a subtle twist. **MAKES 4 SERVINGS**

2½ cups (262 g) old-fashioned rolled oats

Finely grated zest of 1 lemon

Finely grated zest and juice of 1 orange

1½ teaspoons licorice root powder

1 cup (240 g) water

FOR SERVING

2½ cups (625 g) plain yogurt

1 cup (120 g) fresh fruit (I recommend pears or blackberries!)

3 tablespoons runny honey

2 tablespoons finely chopped toasted hazelnuts (see Toasting Nuts and Seeds, page 42)

2 pinches of kosher salt

The day before you plan on enjoying this breakfast treat, you'll want to get the oats soaking. In a medium bowl, stir together the oats, lemon and orange zests, orange juice, licorice root powder, and water. Transfer to a lidded airtight container and refrigerate for at least 5 hours, preferably overnight.

The following day, gently stir the yogurt, fruit (save some for topping), honey, hazelnuts, and salt into the porridge base. Divide among four bowls and serve immediately. The finished overnight oats can be stored in an airtight container in the refrigerator for up to 2 days (after that, the fruit tends to get a little mushy).

Granola
with Chamomile and Dried Blueberries

Owning a restaurant is demanding, and too often I find myself rushing out the door in the morning without breakfast. It's not ideal—I always feel better when I start the day with something nourishing. So sometimes on days off, I make batches of simple, wholesome food to carry me through the week.

Homemade granola, like this one, is one of those staples. Having it on hand means breakfast or an afternoon snack, though brief, is never too difficult to throw together. The addition of chamomile flowers is partially for the plant's calming properties, partly for the pretty appearance. If you have other flaked grains on hand, swap up to ½ cup (52 g) spelt, rye, or barley flakes for the rolled oats. Bob's Red Mill 5 Grain Hot Cereal also works well. Just avoid quick or steel-cut oats, which won't give the right texture. **MAKES 4 SERVINGS**

- 2 tablespoons unsalted butter, melted
- 2 tablespoons runny honey
- 1½ cups (157 g) old-fashioned rolled oats
- ⅓ cup (30 g) walnut pieces, chopped
- 1 teaspoon peeled and finely grated fresh ginger
- ½ teaspoon ground cinnamon
- Pinch of kosher salt
- ¼ cup (45 g) dried blueberries
- 1 tablespoon dried whole chamomile flowers
- Milk or your favorite yogurt and floral runny honey, for serving (optional)

Preheat the oven to 325°F (165°C). Line a baking tray with parchment paper.

In a medium bowl, stir together the butter and honey until well combined. Add the oats, walnuts, ginger, cinnamon, and salt. Stir to combine, then pour onto the prepared baking tray and spread into an even layer. Bake until lightly golden and fragrant, stirring once halfway through, about 25 minutes. Place the tray on a rack and add the dried blueberries and chamomile. Stir to combine. Let the granola cool completely.

Serve with milk or over yogurt with a drizzle of honey, if you like.

The granola can be stored in an airtight container at room temperature for up to 2 weeks.

GROWN

The first time I sailed to Samsø, I had no idea I was about to fall in love—with a way of life, an island, and, most important, its produce. Samsø, a small, sweet island to the east of Denmark's mainland, is a place where time seems to move with the seasons rather than the clock. Once the ferry docked and I stepped ashore, I was struck by the charm of it all: thatched-roofed houses with hollyhocks swaying in the breeze, fishing boats emptying their crate-filled bellies, and small roadside stands dotting every other yard. Each stand overflowed with the island's treasures: tiny, sandy-skinned potatoes, bundles of vibrant asparagus, and rosy stalks of rhubarb.

There was something magical about seeing food in this way, presented so simply and honestly. No glossy packaging or perfectly stacked piles, just produce, fresh from the earth. Samsø's potatoes, I quickly learned, are practically royalty in Scandinavia, their arrival each year a cause for celebration. And how could they not be? The island's sandy soil, coupled with its relatively mild winters, gives Samsø's crops a head start, producing some of the first and finest harvests in all of Denmark.

That first meal I had on Samsø has stayed with me since. We boiled those yellow-fleshed potatoes with a few sprigs of lovage, then tossed them with salt, butter, and chives. The potatoes, no bigger than a quarter, were sweet and earthy, and unlike any I had tasted before. Sitting at a picnic table, surrounded by friends and the island's rugged beauty, I felt completely in tune with the rhythm of the land.

This is what I love most about seasonal produce: It connects us to a specific time and place. In Japan, the calendar is divided into seventy-two micro-seasons, each lasting just five days and marked by a subtle shift in nature: the first budding cherry blossoms, the sprouting of rice, or the return of the fireflies. In Scandinavia, the changes may not be marked with such precision, but the idea is the same. The arrival of Samsø's potatoes, or the first stalks of asparagus, signals more than just a new crop—it signals a moment in time, a shift in the year's rhythm, a reminder to savor what's fleeting and fresh.

Cooking seasonally isn't just about flavor, though that's certainly part of it. It's about working with what the land is offering, letting nature set the menu. It's about celebrating abundance when it's there, preserving it for when it's not, and creating meals that reflect the time of year. That's exactly what the recipes in this chapter are meant to be—scripts to follow when the time is right, when you spot the first asparagus, the first potatoes, or even the last corn of the season at the market. When you intentionally follow the rhythm of the land, food not only becomes more than sustenance—it becomes a celebration of time and place.

Spring's Sun with Pink Peppercorn Vinaigrette

This dish is my interpretation of *solöga,* which translates to "the eye of the sun." A classic Swedish preparation, it's often served at Easter or as part of a summer buffet. Each ingredient is arranged in a ring, with a raw egg yolk placed in the center to mimic the sun. The ingredients vary, sometimes even including Swedish *ansjovis* (sprat fillets, similar to anchovies), and in my version the pink peppercorn vinaigrette and browned butter bring everything together.

Freshness is key, so all the prep work should be done the same day, with plating happening just before serving, with the yolk being added at the very last minute. If the idea of a raw yolk isn't for you, just leave it out—the dish will still be delicious. Serve with crispbread, butter, and a chunk of aged cheese for a meal that simply couldn't be more Swedish. **MAKES 4 SERVINGS**

12 ounces (336 g) creamer potatoes, preferably small and new, scrubbed

8 ounces (224 g) asparagus, woody bottoms broken off

4 hard-boiled eggs (see Perfect Hard-Boiled Eggs, page 154)

1⅓ cups (184 g) medium-diced red radish

2 teaspoons thinly sliced shallot

4 sprigs of dill, stems removed

2 tablespoons sliced fresh chives

4 raw egg yolks

Kosher salt and freshly ground black pepper

½ cup Pink Peppercorn Vinaigrette (page 55)

¼ cup (56 g) unsalted butter

Place the potatoes in a medium pot with water to cover. Salt the water heavily, 2 tablespoons of salt per cup of water. Bring to a boil over medium-high heat. Decrease the heat and let the potatoes simmer until fork-tender, about 15 minutes (time will vary slightly depending on the size of the potatoes). Transfer to a colander to drain and cool to room temperature. Cut the potatoes into ½-inch (1 cm) chunks. Set aside.

Prepare a small ice bath and set it aside. Bring a medium pot of lightly salted water to a boil and add the asparagus. Cook until tender and bright green, about 3 minutes, depending on the size of your asparagus. Plunge into the ice bath until cold, drain, and place on a few paper towels, then cut on the diagonal into ½-inch (1 cm) pieces.

Finely chop all four hard-boiled eggs (or push them through the wires of a kitchen spider strainer).

On four 10-inch (25 cm) plates, arrange the chopped eggs around the plate's edge, in a 9-inch (23 cm) circle. Just inside the egg ring, make a potato ring followed by an asparagus ring. The radish fills the remaining space in the center. Arrange the sliced shallot on top of the vegetables, and garnish—still in a circular pattern—with the dill sprigs and chives. Place one raw yolk on top of the radish in the center of each plate. Lightly season the entire plate with salt and pepper. Drizzle the vinaigrette over each plate (though not on the raw yolk). And last, in a medium skillet over high heat, melt the butter until it has turned a golden brown. Quickly remove from the heat and spoon the brown butter over each ring of potatoes. Serve immediately.

Celery Root, Kale, and Parsley Salad

with Spiced Breadcrumbs and Anchovy Dressing

This salad is all about bold flavors and crunch. Thinly sliced raw celery root and kale bring plenty of texture, and in the best way. Breadcrumbs spiced with fennel, cumin, and coriander add warmth and depth. As for the anchovy dressing, if you don't mention the anchovies, most people won't even notice. Feel free to make the dressing well in advance, but don't dress the salad more than 30 minutes ahead to keep it crisp. **MAKES 4 SERVINGS**

BREADCRUMB TOPPING

- 1 teaspoon fennel seeds
- 1 teaspoon cumin seeds
- 1 teaspoon coriander seeds
- 1 fat slice of sourdough, levain, or seeded artisan loaf (about 4½ ounces / 126 g)
- 1 tablespoon unsalted butter
- 1 tablespoon extra-virgin olive oil
- Pinch of kosher salt

SALAD

- 1 large celery root (1 pound / 454 g), peeled and cut into quarters
- 5 curly purple kale leaves (4 ounces / 120 g)
- ½ cup (20 g) packed fresh flat-leaf parsley leaves, torn if large
- ½ cup (120 g) Garlic Anchovy Dressing (page 57)
- Kosher salt and freshly ground black pepper
- ½ lemon, for squeezing, as needed

Make the topping. In a mortar or spice grinder, coarsely grind together the fennel, cumin, and coriander seeds. Cut off and discard the bread crust, and either by hand or in the food processor, tear or pulse the bread into very small (think spring peas!) pieces. You should have about 1¼ packed cups (90 g).

In a skillet over medium heat, melt the butter with the oil. Add the breadcrumbs and toast, stirring constantly, until golden brown and crisp, 4 to 6 minutes. Add the spices and salt to the breadcrumbs and continue to cook, stirring, until fragrant, about 30 seconds. Transfer to a plate to cool completely.

Make the salad. Using a mandoline (preferred) or vegetable peeler, shave the celery root into thin slices. Stack the slices on top of each other and cut into ½-inch (1 cm) wide ribbons. Transfer to a medium bowl. Strip the kale leaves from the stems. (My dog likes to eat the stems!) Chop the leaves finely. Add to the bowl with the celery root, along with the parsley leaves. Drizzle 2 tablespoons of the dressing over the vegetables, then toss until evenly coated. Add more dressing if you like, or maybe a squeeze of lemon juice. Season with salt and pepper.

Arrange the salad in a shallow serving bowl. Garnish with the breadcrumbs and serve immediately.

Roasted String Beans
with Basil-Pistachio Sauce

String beans are lovely, but the vibrant green sauce that the beans are tossed in is the real star of this dish. While a food processor works, nothing beats the flavor and texture that comes from pounding it by hand with a mortar and pestle. The effort and elbow grease pay off. Make a little extra and serve it with other oven-roasted vegetables like cauliflower or zucchini.

For the beans, seek out the freshest you can find, small to medium in size, with a firm snap. Older, starchier beans will work, especially under the broiler, but they won't have the same sweetness or bite. When the bean season is in full swing, I like to use half green beans and half yellow wax beans to create a stunning presentation. **MAKES 4 SERVINGS**

BASIL-PISTACHIO SAUCE

3 tablespoons toasted pistachios (see Toasting Nuts and Seeds, page 42)

1 garlic clove

Kosher salt and freshly ground black pepper

1 cup (20 g) packed fresh basil leaves, coarsely chopped

½ cup (10 g) packed baby spinach, coarsely chopped

1 teaspoon finely grated lemon zest

¼ cup (14 g) packed freshly grated Parmesan

⅓ cup (73 g) extra-virgin olive oil, plus more as needed

STRING BEANS

8 ounces (224 g) green beans, trimmed

8 ounces (224 g) yellow wax beans (if available, otherwise use more green beans), trimmed

Extra-virgin olive oil

Kosher salt and freshly ground black pepper

½ cup (115 g) crème fraîche, for serving

Make the sauce. In a large mortar, pound the pistachios and garlic into a rough paste. Add a pinch of salt and then begin adding the basil and spinach a handful at a time, crushing the leaves into small pieces against the side of the mortar before adding more. Move the pestle in a circular motion and occasionally use it to push everything down to the bottom again. The optimal consistency at this stage is a creamy paste. Add the lemon zest, followed by the cheese, then, little by little, the olive oil. Season with salt and pepper and adjust the consistency with a little more olive oil if needed. Set aside.

Adjust an oven rack to the closest level under the broiler and preheat the broiler.

Make the string beans. Rinse and pat the beans dry with paper towels, then pile onto a baking tray. Drizzle with olive oil and season lightly with salt. Toss to coat evenly and spread the beans in an even layer. Roast under the broiler, without stirring, until crisp-tender and slightly browned, 3 to 5 minutes. (Timing depends on the size and age of the beans, plus the strength of your broiler.)

Transfer the roasted beans to a bowl and dollop about two-thirds of the sauce onto the beans. Toss to coat and season with salt and pepper. Add more sauce to your liking.

To serve, spread a swoosh of the crème fraîche on a small platter or large plate, or divide among four plates. Top with the dressed beans and serve warm or at room temperature.

CONTINUED

VARIATION

Nasturtium and Kale-Pistachio Sauce

During spring and summer in San Francisco, wild nasturtium seems to cover every green patch in my neighborhood. It's hard to miss, especially when the bright orange and yellow flowers start blooming. I've added the greens into salads before and used the flowers for garnish, but until recently that'd been the extent of it. This variation swaps peppery nasturtium leaves for the basil and tender baby kale for the spinach, giving the sauce a spicier edge. To be perfectly honest, I have a hard time deciding whether I prefer this version or the original, but this one definitely takes the notion of "locally sourced" to a whole new level.

1 cup (20 g) packed fresh nasturtium leaves, coarsely chopped

½ cup (10 g) packed baby kale, coarsely chopped

Follow the original recipe, using nasturtium leaves instead of basil and baby kale instead of baby spinach.

weighing in on organics

As consumers, we make so many choices every time we shop, especially for food. Often, organic ingredients are more expensive than conventional, and it can be difficult to know what the differences are. Here's a brief overview of what you're guaranteed when you shop organic.

Fewer pesticides and additives.

Organic produce is grown without synthetic pesticides and herbicides, which means fewer chemical residues on your food. That's cleaner food for you, better for the farmers, and better for the soil.

Pollination is sustained.

Organic farming helps protect pollinators like bees, butterflies, and other insects. Increased biodiversity lets nature do the work to produce healthy food.

Animals have improved living conditions.

Organic meat and dairy come from animals raised with more space, better diets, and without routine antibiotics or synthetic hormones. It also feels more justifiable to eat an animal raised with respect and care.

Organic foods are often more flavorful.

Organic fruits and vegetables tend to grow at a more natural pace and animals live longer and under better conditions instead of being rushed to maturity with artificial boosters. This time aids in developing deeper flavors.

Swedish Cucumber Salad

I once worked for a chef who forbade two ingredients from ever coming into his kitchen: dill and green peppers. At the time, I respected his wishes, but it'd be difficult for me to agree to such terms today. Dill, fennel, tarragon, and star anise, with their varied anise nuances, have since become essentials in my Scandinavian cooking—I can't do without! This recipe is made creamy with the addition of sour cream, but I've also made it without and instead drizzled in some good olive oil. The salad pairs perfectly with a plate of ripe tomatoes, grilled vegetables (like green peppers, ah!), and roast pork. For a variation, try using shaved fennel instead of cucumber—it's also delightful! **MAKES 2 CUPS**

1½ pounds (672 g) cucumbers (preferably English or Persian)

1 tablespoon kosher salt, plus more as needed

½ medium red onion, thinly sliced (3 ounces / 84 g)

1 small garlic clove, minced

1 cup (250 g) sour cream

2 tablespoons apple cider vinegar

2 tablespoons chopped fresh dill

1 teaspoon sugar

Freshly ground black pepper

Peel the cucumbers lengthwise in a stripe pattern, leaving a strip of unpeeled cucumber between each strip of peeled. Using a mandoline or a very sharp chef's knife, slice the cucumbers into ⅛-inch (3 mm) thick rounds and put in a medium bowl. Sprinkle with the 1 tablespoon of salt and toss to combine. Let sit at room temperature for 30 minutes.

Meanwhile, in a small bowl, stir together the onion, garlic, sour cream, vinegar, dill, and sugar. (Wait on adding more salt because your cucumbers will be bringing some saltiness with them.)

Once the cucumbers are ready, pour off and discard any liquid, pressing gently on the cucumbers to release a few more drops. Pour the dressing over the cucumbers and stir to combine. Season to taste with salt and pepper and keep refrigerated until ready to serve. The salad can be stored in an airtight container in the refrigerator for 3 days.

Warm Potato Salad

with Silken Leeks and Celery Seed Vinaigrette

There's something so comforting about the combination of celery and potatoes. My favorite small potato is called Bintje, a classic Dutch variety, but because they can be hard to find outside of farmers' markets and are only in season for a short time, Yukon golds are a tasty and reliable stand-in.

Lovage, an herbaceous member of the parsley, celery, and carrot family, would be a natural addition, but it can be tricky to find here in the United States. I planted a few seedlings on my back porch a few years ago, but something about the California climate—or maybe my overzealous tending—keeps them from thriving. At any rate, flat-leaf parsley is an excellent substitute, and together with the pale, inner celery stalks you can get pretty close to the lovely lovage flavor. **MAKES 6 SERVINGS**

1¼ pounds (567 g) leeks

¼ cup (60 g) unsalted butter

Kosher salt

3 sprigs of thyme

1½ pounds (680 g) small Bintje or Yukon gold potatoes, scrubbed

4 small inner celery stalks with leaves (3½ ounces / 100 g)

2 tablespoons coarsely chopped fresh lovage or flat-leaf parsley

VINAIGRETTE

6 tablespoons extra-virgin olive oil

¼ cup white wine vinegar

1 tablespoon Dijon mustard

½ teaspoon celery seed

Kosher salt

Trim the leeks to just the white and pale green parts. Halve lengthwise, then cut crosswise into 1-inch (2.5 cm) pieces. Add to a large bowl half full of water and swirl them around and separate the layers to remove any dirt. The leeks will float, and the dirt should sink to the bottom of the bowl.

In a large, heavy-bottomed saucepan over medium heat, melt the butter. Using your hands, remove the leeks from the water and add them to the saucepan (you want some residual water to help sweat the leeks). Season generously with salt and add the thyme sprigs. Stir to combine. When the leeks start to soften, stir again, then decrease the heat to low. Cover and cook, stirring occasionally, until the leeks are very soft and creamy, 15 to 18 minutes. If they start to stick, add a little more water. Transfer the leeks to a large bowl, discard the thyme sprigs, and set aside to cool slightly.

In the same saucepan, add the potatoes, 1 tablespoon salt, and cold water to cover by 1 inch (2.5 cm). Bring to a boil over high heat, then decrease the heat to medium-high and boil gently, stirring occasionally, until the potatoes are very tender but not falling apart, about 12 minutes. Remove from the heat and let them sit in the water for 5 minutes before draining. Return the potatoes to the saucepan, cover, and set aside.

While the potatoes cook, trim the celery leaves from the stalks. Thinly slice the celery stalks; halve any larger parts of the stalk lengthwise and then slice so they are in even pieces. Coarsely chop the celery leaves, keeping a few whole for garnish. Transfer the celery, chopped celery leaves, and lovage to the bowl with the leeks.

Make the vinaigrette. In a jar with a tight-fitting lid, combine the olive oil, vinegar, mustard, celery seed, and a pinch of salt. Cover and shake vigorously until emulsified. Taste and season with more salt if needed.

Cut the potatoes into chunks no larger than 2 inches (5 cm). If they are small, keep them whole. Add the potatoes to the bowl with the leeks. Toss to combine, then drizzle with about 6 tablespoons (90 g) of the vinaigrette. Toss again, taste, and add more vinaigrette and/or salt if needed. Garnish with the reserved leaves, if using. Serve warm.

Carrot and Cauliflower Salad

with Grainy Mustard Yogurt Dressing

When my kids were small and we lived in Copenhagen, getting dinner on the table each day was sometimes a challenge. To make things easier, we subscribed to a weekly fresh vegetable box from a local farm. It was always a fun surprise to see what we were given, but sometimes certain vegetables would pile up faster than we could use them. At one point, faced with an abundance of carrots and cauliflower, I made this salad. A bit like coleslaw but with a tangy yogurt dressing instead of mayonnaise, it's hearty, crunchy, and works beautifully alongside grilled sausage, fish, or even another vegetable salad. **MAKES 6 SERVINGS**

1 small head of cauliflower, tough leaves removed and discarded (1 pound / 454 g after trimming)

3 to 4 medium carrots (8 ounces / 224 g)

Kosher salt

2 tablespoons chopped fresh dill, plus small sprigs for garnish

DRESSING

¾ cup (188 g) plain whole milk yogurt

1 tablespoon plus 1 teaspoon whole grain mustard

1½ teaspoons Dijon mustard

1½ teaspoons runny honey

½ teaspoon coriander seeds, crushed in a mortar and pestle

Kosher salt and freshly ground black pepper

Cut off the stem of the cauliflower, then cut the stem into quarters lengthwise. Very thinly slice the stem crosswise. Transfer to a large bowl.

Break up the cauliflower into florets. Thinly slice any long stems, then chop the florets into small florets. Transfer to the bowl.

Trim, scrub, and shred the carrots in the large holes of a box grater. Transfer to the bowl with the cauliflower.

Season with salt and add the chopped dill, then toss to evenly distribute.

Make the dressing. In a small bowl, whisk together the yogurt, both mustards, the honey, and crushed coriander seeds. Add to the vegetable mixture and toss to coat evenly. Season with salt and pepper. Transfer to a bowl, cover, and refrigerate for at least an hour and up to one day before garnishing with fresh dill and serving.

Red Cabbage–Endive Salad

with Autumn Fruits and Pumpkin Seeds

This salad reminds me of autumn and all the produce that comes with it—apples, cabbage, oranges, and bitter greens. In Scandinavia, red cabbage and endive are usually eaten during the December holidays, but I like having a way to enjoy them outside that time. The apple cider vinaigrette, with orange zest and crushed pink peppercorns, brings warmth and brightness.

I have always loved the combination of cabbage and fruit. When we lived in Copenhagen, I would often buy whole heads of red cabbage at the market, thinking I'd use them up quickly. Inevitably, they would last a lot longer, lingering in the fridge until a salad like this gave them a second life. **MAKES 4 TO 6 SERVINGS**

DRESSING

1 tablespoon minced shallot

2 tablespoons apple cider vinegar

1 teaspoon finely grated orange zest (from 1 orange)

2 tablespoons fresh orange juice

1 teaspoon Dijon mustard

1 teaspoon maple syrup

Pinch of kosher salt

½ teaspoon pink peppercorns, crushed lightly

¼ cup (55 g) extra-virgin olive oil

SALAD

2 navel oranges

2 cups (180 g) finely shredded red cabbage

1 small radicchio (red endive), halved, cored, and thinly sliced crosswise (4 ounces / 112 g)

1 green endive or green speckled radicchio, halved, cored, and cut on a bias into ¼-inch (6 mm) slices (4½ ounces / 126 g)

1 pink apple, cored, halved lengthwise, and very thinly sliced crosswise

4 ounces (115 g) dried figs, stemmed and coarsely chopped

Kosher salt and freshly ground black pepper

¼ cup (40 g) toasted pumpkin seeds (see Toasting Nuts and Seeds, page 42)

4 ounces (115 g) creamy blue cheese (such as Danish Blue), crumbled

Make the dressing. In a jar with a tight-fitting lid, combine the shallot and vinegar. Set aside for 15 minutes to macerate. Add the orange zest and juice, mustard, maple syrup, salt, and pink peppercorns. Cover and shake to combine. Add the oil, cover, and shake vigorously until emulsified. (Alternatively, make the dressing using a bowl and whisk, whisking the oil in slowly at the end until the mixture emulsifies.)

Make the salad. Using a small sharp knife, cut a slice off both ends of each orange to reveal the flesh. Stand one orange upright on a cutting board and slice off the peel (including the white pith) in strips, following the contour of the fruit. Holding the orange in one hand over a bowl, cut along either side of each segment to release it from the membrane, letting them drop into the bowl. Repeat with the second orange.

In a large, wide serving bowl, toss together the cabbage, radicchio, and endive. Drizzle with a little dressing and toss to coat evenly. Add the orange segments, apple slices, and figs and toss gently to combine. Season with salt and pepper. Top with the pumpkin seeds and blue cheese. Drizzle with more dressing and serve.

Kale and Einkorn Salad

with Mirabelles and Walnut Vinaigrette

Mirabelle trees are common in Scandinavia, and lucky me, my neighbor has a big one in her yard here in San Francisco. When the fruit ripens, the sidewalk below is scattered with purplish plums, small enough to be mistaken for cherries. Their firm, sweet flesh and slightly tart skin make them perfect for salads like this one. If you don't have mirabelles, plums work well too.

Einkorn, an ancient wheat, adds a hearty chew and makes the salad into a substantial meal. Its name comes from the German words *ein* (one) and *korn* (grain), since each wheat spikelet holds just one single wheat grain as opposed to modern wheats, which often yield three to four times that amount. As one of the earliest cultivated wheats, it has a nutty depth that pairs beautifully with the walnut vinaigrette. The squeeze of lemon added at the end really brightens everything up. **MAKES 4 SERVINGS**

⅔ cup (130 g) einkorn

4 cups (320 g) stemmed and finely chopped kale

2 large radicchio leaves, torn into bite-size pieces

12 mirabelles, or 4 small plums, halved and sliced (6 ounces / 168 g)

¼ cup (60 g) Walnut Vinaigrette (page 56)

Kosher salt and freshly ground black pepper

½ lemon, for squeezing, as needed

1 tablespoon toasted walnut pieces (see Toasting Nuts and Seeds, page 42)

Mustard flowers, nasturtium, or sorrel (sour grass) flowers, for garnish

Put the einkorn into a small saucepan and add water to cover by about 1 inch (2.5 cm). Bring to a boil, add a pinch of salt, then decrease the heat to medium. Simmer gently, adding a bit more water while cooking if the water goes below the surface of the einkorn, until the einkorn is soft yet still chewy, 35 to 40 minutes. Drain in a colander and let the grains cool. (The einkorn can be made in advance and kept in an airtight container in the refrigerator for up to 4 days.)

In a large bowl, combine the kale, radicchio, mirabelles, cooked einkorn, and dressing, along with a pinch of salt and pepper. Use your hands to mix it all together, gently rubbing the leaves to make sure the dressing gets into the small curls of the kale. Squeeze some lemon juice onto the greens and toss again. Season the salad with more salt and pepper, and give it a final toss.

Divide the salad among four shallow bowls, sprinkle with the toasted walnuts and edible flowers, and serve immediately.

Shaved Melon and Spinach Salad with Feta

A few years ago, my staff and I made this salad for a magical outdoor dinner in Sonoma, where more than 175 guests sat at one incredibly long table in the middle of a vineyard. It had been a hot day, and, as the evening cooled, this refreshing salad was served at just the right time. Tender spinach, juicy melon, creamy feta, tart lemon, and toasted seeds—it was so simple, but it was what everyone was in the mood for!

The long, silky ribbons of melon make this salad feel luxurious, and without a doubt, the best way to slice them is with a mandoline. Take your time and hold the melon with a paper towel to keep it from slipping out of your grip. If you don't have a mandoline, a Y-peeler works well, or you can slice the melon as thinly as possible with a chef's knife. The goal is to make a delicious salad, not to harm yourself. I believe in you! **MAKES 4 SERVINGS**

1 small cantaloupe or other fresh, fragrant melon (1½ pounds / 680 g), peeled

4 to 5 ounces (112 to 140 g) baby spinach

1 tablespoon fresh lemon or lime juice, or as needed

3 ounces (84 g) sheep's milk feta cheese, crumbled

Extra-virgin olive oil

¼ cup (35 g) 4-Seed Sprinkle (page 42)

Flaky sea salt (such as Maldon), for garnish

Trim the ends from the melon and halve lengthwise. Scoop out and discard the seeds. Cut the melon lengthwise into six wedges. Carefully slice the melon as thinly as possible on the mandoline, without causing the melon ribbons to break into smaller pieces. (If using a peeler, "peel" the melon into long ribbon-like strips.) Stack neatly on a plate until all the melon has been sliced.

In a large bowl, toss the spinach with the lemon juice. Arrange the spinach on a large platter, then gently place the melon ribbons around on the salad in swirls and curls. Sprinkle with the feta, then drizzle with olive oil. Garnish with the seed mix and a sprinkle of flaky salt. Serve at once.

Chunked Cabbage and Cottage Cheese Salad

Arrowhead cabbage—a type of cabbage with a head shaped like a cone—is mild and surprisingly sweet. When my kids were small, I used to set out a bowl of raw chunks of it while they watched TV, and they would gnaw on it happily. I tried the same trick with my now teenagers—not a chance. But come dinnertime, they were at least willing to eat some of the salad.

Cilantro isn't a typical Scandinavian herb, but in this instance, I love how it brightens up cabbage with a fresh, lemony kick. If cilantro isn't your thing, parsley or dill works, too. For the best texture, make this salad no more than an hour before serving. If you're unable to find arrowhead cabbage, go with green or red cabbage instead. **MAKES 6 SERVINGS**

1 medium arrowhead, green, or red cabbage (about 1½ pounds / 680 g), outer leaves and core removed

⅔ cup (175 g) whole milk cottage cheese

2 tablespoons fresh lemon juice

1 tablespoon olive oil

¼ cup chopped fresh cilantro, flat-leaf parsley, or dill

1 teaspoon poppy seeds

Kosher salt and freshly ground black pepper

Cut the cabbage into 1-inch (2.5 cm) cubes, allowing the layers to stick together if they want. In a large bowl, stir together the cottage cheese, lemon juice, and olive oil. Add the cabbage, cilantro, and poppy seeds and toss to evenly coat. Season with salt and black pepper. Serve at once or refrigerate for up to 1 hour before serving.

Spice-Roasted Beet, Winter Squash, and Fennel Salad

In this vibrant salad, beets and squash are roasted with a fragrant blend of fennel, coriander, and cumin seeds, which deepens their earthy sweetness. Once roasted, crisp raw fennel is tossed in, bringing freshness and crunch to balance the softer textures. Yes, we're leaving the skins of both beets and kuri squash on, as they are completely edible—just give them a good scrub first (see page 37 on the essential green scrubby). **MAKES 4 TO 6 SERVINGS**

1½ pounds (680 g) red, golden, or Chioggia beets or a mixture, scrubbed

1 small red kuri (Hokkaido) or butternut squash (1½ to 1¾ pounds / 680 to 795 g), scrubbed

1 teaspoon fennel seeds

1 teaspoon coriander seeds

1 teaspoon cumin seeds

1 tablespoon kosher salt

Extra-virgin olive oil

1 small fennel bulb (about 7 ounces / 200 g)

¼ cup (60 g) Basic Vinaigrette (page 54), or more as desired

Fresh dill and, if available, fennel fronds, for garnish

Preheat the oven to 425°F (220°C). Line two large baking trays with parchment paper.

Lightly trim the bottom and top off each beet. Then cut each beet into ½-inch (1 cm) thick slices horizontally. Transfer to a baking tray and arrange in a single layer.

If using red kuri squash, halve it lengthwise. Trim the ends, then scoop out and discard the seeds and fibrous membrane with a metal spoon. Cut the squash into ½-inch (1 cm) wide pieces. If using butternut, peel the entire squash and then cut in two widthwise, right where the skinnier top meets the round bottom, and then cut the bottom half in half lengthwise. Scoop out and discard the seeds and fibrous membrane with a metal spoon, then into ½-inch (1 cm) pieces. (The top portion of the butternut can be cut horizontally into ½-inch / 1 cm disks.) Spread out on the second baking tray in an even layer.

In a mortar or spice grinder, combine the fennel seeds, coriander seeds, cumin seeds, and salt and grind into a rough powder. Drizzle the beets and the squash with olive oil, followed by the spice blend.

Roast until the vegetables are tender and lightly browned but not mushy, rotating the baking trays halfway through from top to bottom and front to back, 30 to 40 minutes. Set aside to cool to room temperature.

While the vegetables roast, prepare the fennel. Cut off the top fronds, if there are any (saving some for garnish). Holding the root end of the bulb, shave the fennel crosswise on a mandoline. Alternatively, cut the bulb in half lengthwise and slice as thinly as possible with a chef's knife. Transfer the fennel to a bowl. Drizzle with the vinaigrette and toss gently to coat.

Arrange the beets and squash on a large platter, starting with a large layer on the bottom and piling up in the middle with each additional layer. Top with the shaved fennel and more vinaigrette if needed. Garnish with fresh dill and fronds and serve at once.

Butter Lettuce, Herb, and Nut Salad

Before you even ask, yes, the amount of herbs in the ingredient list is correct. Using them this generously is what makes this salad so special. It was inspired by Ottolenghi's Soft Herb Salad with brown butter and almonds—the one with no lettuce whatsoever, just herbs. Chervil, with its feathery leaves and delicate anise flavor, can be tricky to find, so if you can't get it, just use more of the other herbs. If you like the idea of foraging, chickweed or lamb's quarters would be great additions, as well as colorful edible flowers (see A Forager at Heart, page 239). **MAKES 4 SERVINGS**

4 heads of butterhead lettuce (such as Bibb or Boston) (about 1½ pounds / 680 g)

4 firmly packed cups (80g) fresh soft herb leaves (such as flat-leaf parsley, chervil, tarragon, mint, and dill)

1 bunch of chives, cut into ½-inch (1 cm) segments

⅓ cup Mormor Dressing (page 56)

Freshly ground black pepper

1 cup (140 g) Spiced Crushed Nuts (page 43)

Place four plates on the work surface.

Remove and discard any wilted or damaged outer lettuce leaves. Break the remaining leaves apart and wash them thoroughly. Pat them dry gently.

Pour the dressing into a large bowl and give it a quick five-stroke whisk to make it frothy again. Start by taking a large lettuce leaf and dipping it right side up in the dressing. Wipe it up along the inside of the bowl and then hold it momentarily over the bowl to let any excess dressing drip off. (The dressing isn't meant to coat the backside of the lettuce.) Place the leaf dressing side up, just off-center on one of the plates. Repeat with the next seven largest leaves so that you have two leaves on each plate, placed in a way that begins to "rebuild" the shape of the lettuce head again.

Sprinkle a pinch of herbs over the lettuce on each plate and then continue with the next largest eight leaves, dipping in dressing and arranging on the plate on top of the first two leaves. After each pair of lettuce leaves is added to a plate, follow with more herbs. Continue working in this fashion—lettuce leaves getting smaller and smaller—until all the lettuce and herbs have been used. Top with a grind of pepper and a shower of crushed nuts. Serve immediately.

Broccoli-Avocado Salad

with Horseradish

Raw broccoli salads have never been my thing until I created this version. By using both the head and peeled stem, there's hardly any waste, and the result is all crunch and flavor. This is the kind of salad you can prep a day ahead and then mix just before serving. That way, the avocado keeps its bright green color and the broccoli keeps its bite. The freshness is enhanced even more by the lively sprouts on top. **MAKES 6 SERVINGS**

1 large head of broccoli (about 12 ounces / 336 g)

1 tablespoon extra-virgin olive oil, plus more for garnish

4 teaspoons fresh lemon juice, plus more as needed

Kosher salt and freshly ground black pepper

⅓ cup (83 g) sour cream

2 tablespoons peeled and finely grated fresh horseradish, plus more for garnish

2 avocados, cut into 1-inch (2.5 cm) chunks

3 to 5 ounces (84 to 140 g) sprouts (such as mung bean or chickpea)

Cut the broccoli head off the stem. Using a peeler, peel the tough outer layer on the stem, discarding the trimmings. Using a sharp chef's knife, slice the broccoli stem crosswise into ⅛-inch (3 mm) thick slices. Place into a medium bowl. Using a very sharp chef's knife, slice the broccoli head into thin slices (it's okay if some are just small green bits). Add to the bowl with the sliced stems. Add the olive oil and 3 teaspoons of the lemon juice and season with salt and pepper. Toss the salad carefully to avoid roughing up the broccoli pieces more than necessary.

In a small bowl, stir together the sour cream, horseradish, and the remaining 1 teaspoon lemon juice. Season with salt and pepper.

Arrange the dressed broccoli in a large, shallow bowl and garnish with spoonfuls of the horseradish dressing, avocado chunks, more shredded horseradish, the sprouts, and a last drizzle of olive oil. Serve immediately.

Roasted Sunchokes

with Dandelion Greens, Almonds, and Rye Crackers

Sunchokes, also known as Jerusalem artichokes, are naturally sweet when raw and even more so after roasting. In this recipe, that sweetness meets the pleasant bitterness of dandelion greens, and everything is tied together with a lively preserved lemon vinaigrette. Toasted almonds and rye crackers add a nutty crunch.

If sunchokes are hard to find, celery root or parsnip makes a great substitute. And if you like the idea of foraging, harvesting your own dandelion greens could be pretty rad (see A Forager at Heart, page 239). **MAKES 4 TO 6 SERVINGS**

ALMONDS

½ cup (75 g) whole almonds

1 tablespoon unsalted butter

Kosher salt and freshly ground black pepper

ROASTED SUNCHOKES

2 pounds (900 g) sunchokes (Jerusalem artichokes), scrubbed and cut into 1½-inch (4 cm) chunks

Extra-virgin olive oil

4 very thin slices sprouted rye bread (rugbrød)

1 cup (240 g) Preserved Lemon Vinaigrette (page 58)

1 bunch of fresh dandelion greens or arugula (about 5 ounces / 140 g), trimmed and torn into pieces

Preheat the oven to 425°F (220°C).

Prepare the almonds. Fill a small saucepan halfway with water and bring to a boil over high heat. Add the almonds and boil for 30 to 45 seconds (do not overcook or the almonds will become soft). Drain in a fine-mesh sieve, then run cold water over the almonds to stop the cooking. Squeeze each almond between your fingers to slip off the skins. Discard the skins and set the almonds aside.

In a small skillet over medium heat, melt the butter. Add the almonds and a pinch of salt and cook, stirring constantly, until golden brown and fragrant, about 3 minutes. Season with another pinch of salt. Transfer to a plate and let cool completely. When cool, coarsely chop the almonds and set aside.

Prepare the sunchokes. Pile the sunchokes on a baking tray and drizzle with olive oil. Season with salt and pepper and toss to coat evenly. Spread into an even layer. Roast, stirring and turning once, until tender and golden, about 30 minutes. Transfer the roasted sunchokes to a small platter or wide serving bowl and let cool to room temperature.

While the sunchokes cool, decrease the oven temperature to 350°F (175°C). Lightly brush the rye bread slices on both sides with olive oil, then sprinkle with salt. Arrange in a single layer on a baking tray and bake, turning once halfway through, until browned and crisp, 18 to 22 minutes. Remove from the oven and set aside to cool; the bread will crisp up further as it cools.

Drizzle the sunchokes with 2 tablespoons of the vinaigrette. Add the dandelion greens and most of the almonds. Drizzle with a little more vinaigrette and toss to combine. Break the rye crackers into large pieces and sprinkle over the salad. Garnish with the remaining almonds and serve, passing the vinaigrette alongside.

LUNCH-ISH

For years, when I lived in Copenhagen, every Friday after work, my husband and I would pack the car—kids in the back seat, a filled cooler wedged between bags—and drive across the Öresund Bridge to our summerhouse in southern Sweden. Surrounded by dense forest and far from any neighbors, it was our retreat from city life. We'd arrive just before dusk, light the wood-burning stove, and make a simple dinner before slipping between the still-chilly sheets for the night.

The next morning, we'd wake with no real plan except to be outside. My introduction to the Scandinavian outdoors happened during those weekends with my family—packing a picnic basket and heading to the lake to swim, or hiking deep into the woods in search of chanterelles and trumpet mushrooms. No matter what we were doing, lunch always came early. Not only because we'd gotten hungry, but also because we were excited to have a picnic out in the wild.

The Norwegian concept of *friluftsliv,* or "free-air life," encourages connecting with nature daily, and it's a notion that is embraced throughout Scandinavia. In Danish winters, babies are bundled into carriages and left to nap outdoors, the fresh air believed to keep them healthy. Many children attend *skovbørnehaver*—forest kindergarten—where they spend most of their day outside, playing, learning, and eating, sometimes near a bonfire for warmth and *hygge.* In Norway, there are government-sponsored "libraries" where anyone can borrow outdoor gear, and throughout Scandinavia many employers encourage their staff to step away from their desks midday, go outside, and move their bodies. It all plays into the idea that we should work to live, not live to work, something I've come to appreciate deeply. It's a rather unconventional kind of sustainability, one that nourishes both people and the planet.

In Norway and Sweden, there is a centuries-old principle called *Allemannsretten,* "the right to roam," that allows people to hike, camp, and explore almost anywhere—even private property—as long as they respect nature and local communities. (Sadly, Denmark doesn't have the same legal right, though there are still lots of trails, beaches, and green spaces to enjoy.)

The recipes in this chapter are suitable to be made in big batches, meant to be packed into a lunch box or tucked into a backpack. They taste just as good in the open air as they do at a work desk, as part of a smörgåsbord spread, or on the dinner table. Kamut and Corn Salad with Avocado and Saffron Vinaigrette (page 144) has made me even more of a lover of fragrant saffron. And whenever I pack Chanterelle, Charred Corn, and Goat Cheese Tartlets (page 155) into my bag, I'm instantly transported to a picnic blanket deep in a Swedish forest, savoring the bounty of our edible "gold rush" from the previous day's forage with my family.

Chard and Farmers Cheese Tart

with Dark Rye Crust

When I lived in Copenhagen, I had a backyard greenhouse and garden where rhubarb, lovage, and an array of greens grew. The first time I made this tart was after harvesting a big bunch of chard from there, the leaves vibrant and full of life. Now that I live in San Francisco without a garden, I rely on getting chard at the farmers' market, where during the season, it comes in every color imaginable.

If you can't find chard, sautéed baby spinach or sliced cooked beets (with the same raw weight as the chard) work well, too—just be sure to squeeze out any excess liquid from the spinach before adding it to the unbaked crust. I love the slight crunch that rye grits add to the crust. For a crisper crust, blind bake it with pie weights for about 15 minutes at 350°F (175°C) before filling, keeping in mind that doing so will reduce the final bake time by 10 to 15 minutes.

MAKES ONE 9½-INCH (24 CM) TART

CRUST

1 cup (120 g) rye flour

½ cup (64 g) all-purpose flour

1 tablespoon rye grits or old-fashioned rolled oats

2 tablespoons plain whole milk yogurt

⅓ cup (75 g) unsalted butter, at room temperature

1 teaspoon kosher salt

1 to 2 tablespoons ice water

CUSTARD FILLING

4 eggs

1 cup (240 g) heavy cream

¼ teaspoon kosher salt, plus more as needed

2 tablespoons grated semihard or hard cheese (such as aged Gouda or Parmesan)

2 tablespoons chopped fresh chives

CHARD

1 tablespoon extra-virgin olive oil

1 tablespoon minced shallot

Make the crust. In a medium bowl, stir the rye and all-purpose flours, rye grits, yogurt, butter, and salt together with your fingertips until combined. Add 1 tablespoon of the ice water to help bring the dough together. If necessary, you can add up to the remaining tablespoon. Wrap the dough in parchment paper or plastic wrap and refrigerate for at least 30 minutes.

While the dough chills, make the custard filling. In a medium bowl, whisk together the eggs, cream, salt, grated cheese, and chives.

Once you are ready to roll out your crust, preheat the oven to 350°F (175°C). Have ready a 9½-inch (24 cm) tart pan.

Lightly dust a work surface with flour and roll the chilled dough into a 12-inch (30 cm) round. To transfer the dough to the tart pan, gently curl it around your rolling pin—this makes the dough easier to carry to the pan without it breaking. Uncurl it from the rolling pin directly over the pan and carefully press it down into the bottom and against the sides of the pan. Use your fingertip or a chef's knife to trim any overhang and use the scraps to repair any cracks or holes to prevent seepage. Refrigerate the tart pan while you prepare the chard.

Prepare the chard. In a medium skillet over medium heat, warm the olive oil. Add the shallot and chard stems and cook, stirring occasionally, until both have softened, 3 to 4 minutes. Add the chard leaves and stir continuously until they just begin to wilt.

CONTINUED

1 large bunch of chard (about 7 ounces / 196 g), stems and leaves separated, stems chopped, leaves left in large pieces

¼ cup (65 g) Farmers Cheese (page 82) or goat cheese

Kosher salt and freshly ground black pepper

Place the refrigerated tart pan on a baking tray and transfer the mixture immediately to the pan, making sure to distribute it evenly on the bottom. Gently pour the custard filling into the crust—I like how it looks when some of the chard leaves stick up out of the custard a bit. Drop teaspoon-size clumps of farmers cheese around the top of the tart and finish with a light sprinkle of salt and pepper.

Bake until the custard has firmed up, is slightly puffed, and the edges of the crust are light brown, 40 to 50 minutes. Let the tart cool to room temperature before cutting it into slices.

This tart tastes best the day it is baked but can be stored, wrapped, in the refrigerator for 2 days. Reheat in a 350°F (175°C) oven for 6 to 8 minutes.

Mung Bean Fritters with Goat Cheese

If you've never cooked with the legume called mung beans, now is the time. They are creamy and filling, similar to black beans, and packed with protein, essential amino acids, antioxidants, and nutrients that may help lower blood pressure and LDL cholesterol. A superfood, I'd say. The beans and the fritter base come together quite quickly, and the addition of nutritional yeast deepens the savory flavor, making these fritters even more delectable.

I love taking a few of these on a hike or down to the beach—no utensils needed. The creamy goat cheese tucked inside is a perfect contrast to the crispy exterior, making them just as good warm as they are at room temperature. **MAKES 24 CAKES**

1 pound (454 g) dried mung beans

Kosher salt and freshly ground black pepper

2 medium carrots, scrubbed (5 ounces / 140 g)

2 tablespoons neutral oil, plus more for frying

2 medium onions, finely chopped (12 ounces / 340 g)

2 garlic cloves, minced

2 eggs

½ cup (64 g) all-purpose flour, plus more as needed

½ cup (52 g) quick oats

1 tablespoon nutritional yeast

10 sprigs of flat-leaf parsley, leaves finely chopped

5 sprigs of thyme, stemmed and leaves finely chopped

1 cup (236 g) goat cheese

Place the beans in a medium saucepan and add water to cover by 2 inches (5 cm). Bring to a boil, add a pinch of salt, and decrease the heat to low. Cook gently until the beans are tender and skins have begun to slip off, 30 to 40 minutes, skimming off any impurities that form on the surface and adding more water if needed. Drain in a colander and let cool to room temperature.

Shred the carrots on the large holes of a box grater. Heat the oil in a medium skillet over medium heat. Add the carrots, onions, and garlic and cook until the vegetables are translucent and tender, 5 minutes. Remove the pan from the heat, transfer the vegetables to a large bowl to cool to room temperature, and wipe out the skillet.

Once the beans and the vegetables are cool, pour the beans into the bowl with the vegetables. Add the eggs, flour, oats, nutritional yeast, herbs, 2 teaspoons salt, and a few grinds of pepper. With your hands (my preferred tool!) or a spoon, stir to combine.

I always fry off a small sample before frying an entire batch of a mixture to make sure the seasonings are on point. Heat the skillet over medium heat, add a few drops of oil, and brown a tablespoon-size amount of the mung bean mixture on both sides until cooked through, 1 to 2 minutes. Let cool slightly. Taste and add more salt or pepper to the main batch, if necessary, and if the mixture needs to hold together more, add a tablespoon or so more flour. Fry off another sample, if necessary.

Line a baking tray with parchment paper and portion the mixture into mounds weighing about 2½ ounces (70 g) each. Roll a mound into a ball in your hand and make a depression in the middle with two fingers. Insert a small ball (about 2 teaspoons) of goat cheese into the depression and gently close the mixture around it. Shape into a cake about 2½ inches (6.5 cm) in width. Repeat with the remaining cakes.

CONTINUED

Return the skillet to medium heat. Add enough oil to just barely cover the bottom of the pan. Heat the oil briefly and, working in batches, add the cakes to the pan. Once your pan is full, decrease the heat to medium-low, adjusting it as necessary to find the sweet spot where the cakes cook through without getting too brown on the outside. They should take 2 to 3 minutes to cook on each side. Transfer the cooked cakes to an oven-safe dish. (It's a good idea to keep them warm in a 190°F / 90°C oven while you finish frying.) Cook the remaining cakes in the same fashion, adding more oil as necessary to encourage the formation of a nice crust. Serve immediately.

The cooked cakes can be stored in an airtight container in the refrigerator for 3 days and reheated in a 350°F (175°C) oven for about 10 minutes.

Smashed Cauliflower and Black Lentils
with Curry Cream

Black lentils, sometimes called beluga lentils, are round like pearls (or fish roe) rather than flat, like other lentil varieties. They require no soaking, and I always dress them while still warm as they seem to better absorb the flavors like that. Here, they're paired with golden roasted cauliflower and a creamy spiced curry sauce, making for a visually striking dish: the deep yellow of the curry, the earthy lentils, and the caramelized cauliflower all playing beautifully off each other. This is one of those dishes that I secretly hope will leave enough for leftovers. **MAKES 6 SERVINGS**

LENTILS

¾ cup (150 g) black lentils

1 bay leaf

2 tablespoons apple cider vinegar

2 tablespoons extra-virgin olive oil

Kosher salt and freshly ground black pepper

CAULIFLOWER

2 pounds (900 g) cauliflower florets, about 2 inches (5 cm) each, including some stem

3 tablespoons olive oil

Kosher salt and freshly ground black pepper

About ½ cup (125 g) Curry Cream (page 63)

½ cup (15 g) packed fresh flat-leaf parsley leaves, torn

Preheat the oven to 400°F (200°C).

Make the lentils. In a medium saucepan, combine the lentils, 2 cups water, and the bay leaf. Bring to a boil over high heat. Decrease the heat to low, cover, and simmer until the lentils are tender but not mushy, 15 to 20 minutes, adding more water if necessary. Drain any excess liquid, discard the bay leaf, and pour the lentils into a medium bowl. Add the vinegar and olive oil, season with salt and pepper, and toss to coat. Set aside.

Make the cauliflower. In a large bowl, toss the cauliflower florets with the olive oil, salt, and pepper, then spread out on a baking tray. (I normally don't line the tray with anything because the cauliflower seems to get better color without.)

Roast until the florets are just beginning to color on the bottom, about 15 minutes. Remove the baking tray from the oven and, using tongs, flip the florets. Return the tray to the oven and roast for 15 more minutes. Remove the tray from the oven again, increase the temperature to 450°F (230°C), and then flatten each floret with the backside of a spatula, so they are about ½ inch (1 cm) thick. Put the tray back in the oven and roast until golden and crispy, 10 to 12 minutes more.

To serve, spread half of the curry cream on the bottom of a serving platter, followed by spoonfuls of about half the lentils—be sure to leave some of the curry cream visible. Arrange the cauliflower on top, followed by the rest of the lentils. Garnish with the parsley and serve the remaining curry cream in a small bowl on the side.

Leftovers can be stored in an airtight container in the refrigerator for up to 3 days.

Kamut and Corn Salad

with Avocado and Saffron Vinaigrette

This vibrant and hearty salad is an edible ray of sunshine, thanks to the golden hue from the saffron vinaigrette. Make it when local corn is in season. (In a pinch, frozen corn works, too—no need to thaw first—but fresh will always have the best flavor.) I prefer to cut kernels off the cob over a bowl or rimmed baking tray, to keep them from flying to all sides (well, at least not as much, anyway!).

Kamut (Khorasan wheat) is an ancient grain in the same family as spelt, einkorn, and emmer (farro). It is known for its irresistible chewiness and nutty flavor. The toasted corn kernels have a similar chew, making this salad oh so satisfying to eat! **MAKES 4 TO 6 SERVINGS**

- ⅔ cup (130 g) kamut
- Kosher salt and freshly ground black pepper
- 2 tablespoons extra-virgin olive oil
- ¾ cup (105 g) finely diced onion
- 2½ cups (325 g) fresh corn kernels
- 1½ cups (75 g) chopped red cabbage
- 2 medium avocados, cut into 1-inch (2.5 cm) chunks
- ½ cup (120 g) Saffron Vinaigrette (page 54)

Put the kamut into a small saucepan and add water to cover by about 1 inch (2.5 cm). Bring to a boil, add a pinch of salt, then decrease the heat to medium and simmer until the kamut is soft yet still chewy, 35 to 40 minutes, adding a bit more water as necessary. Remove from the heat and drain in a colander. Set aside as you prepare the rest of the salad. (The kamut can be made in advance and kept in an airtight container in the refrigerator for 4 days.)

In a large skillet over medium heat, warm the olive oil. Add the onion and cook until translucent, about 3 minutes. Add the corn and cook, stirring occasionally, until it just begins to brown, about 5 minutes. Pour into a large bowl and, while still warm, toss with the cooked kamut, cabbage, avocado chunks, and vinaigrette. Season with salt and pepper and serve immediately.

Leftovers can be stored in an airtight container in the refrigerator for up to 3 days.

Chicken Meatballs
with Tarragon Cream

For Valentine's Day one year, I packed a picnic basket for my partner and me to enjoy in Golden Gate Park. Inside was a container of these meatballs with sauce, another of Warm Potato Salad with Silken Leeks and Celery Seed Vinaigrette (page 112), and a chunk of Green's Bread (page 235). We sat in the grass, the sun shining through the treetops, enjoying a peaceful meal, though we were somewhat distracted by our dog Charlie, who kept his gaze locked on the meatballs the entire time!

These meatballs are a mix of dark and white meat, which keeps them juicy and flavorful. If you have a meat grinder, use it here for an even better texture. Try spreading the tarragon cream on a slice of rye bread, top it with a layer of halved meatballs, and you have an open-faced sandwich, a.k.a. smørrebrød, worth savoring. Cooked meatballs freeze beautifully, so I always make a big batch to store for quick meals later. **MAKES 30 MEATBALLS**

MEATBALLS

- 3 medium carrots (7½ ounces / 210 g), scrubbed, cut into 1-inch (2.5 cm) pieces
- 2 medium zucchini (13 ounces / 360 g), cut into 1-inch (2.5 cm) pieces
- 1¾ pounds (795 g) boneless, skinless chicken thighs, cut into 1-inch (2.5 cm) pieces
- 10 ounces (280 g) boneless, skinless chicken breast, cut into 1-inch (2.5 cm) pieces
- Kosher salt and freshly ground black pepper
- 3 medium shallots (3 ounces / 84 g), finely chopped
- 2 garlic cloves, minced
- 2 eggs
- ¼ cup (60 g) whole milk
- ¼ cup (32 g) all-purpose flour, plus more as needed
- Neutral oil, for frying

Make the meatballs. In a food processor, process the carrots and zucchini, pulsing until finely chopped and stopping to scrape down the sides of the bowl a few times. Pour into a colander set in a large bowl and push to expel any excess liquid; discard the liquid. You should have about 2 packed cups (400 g) of vegetables.

Place the food processor bowl back on the machine (no need to wash first). Add the chicken and pulse to chop the meat finely.

Transfer the chopped meat to the bowl of a stand mixer fitted with the paddle attachment. Add 1 tablespoon salt and 2 teaspoons pepper. Beat on medium-high speed until tacky, about 2 minutes. Add the chopped carrots and zucchini, shallots, and garlic and mix to combine. Add the eggs and milk, mix, then add the flour and mix until combined. Cover and refrigerate for 30 minutes. The meat base can be made ahead and kept refrigerated up to 1 day prior to frying.

I always fry off a small sample before frying an entire batch of a mixture to make sure the seasonings are on point. Heat a medium skillet over medium heat, add a few drops of oil, and brown a tablespoon-size patty of the meat mixture on both sides, until cooked through, 1 to 2 minutes per side. Let cool slightly. Taste and add more salt and pepper to the main batch, as needed, and if the mixture needs to hold together more, add a tablespoon or so more flour. Fry off another sample, if necessary.

CONTINUED

TARRAGON CREAM

¼ cup (15 g) chopped fresh tarragon leaves (from about 2 bunches)

5 tablespoons (78 g) sour cream

2 tablespoons mayonnaise

2 teaspoons fresh lemon juice

1 teaspoon Dijon mustard

Kosher salt and freshly ground black pepper

Make the tarragon cream. In a small bowl, mix the tarragon, sour cream, mayonnaise, lemon juice, and mustard. Season with salt and pepper. You should be able to taste the tarragon as well as the zing from the lemon juice and mustard. Cover and refrigerate until ready to serve. The cream can be made ahead and kept refrigerated up to 2 days prior to serving.

Preheat the oven to 190°F (90°C). Line a baking tray with parchment paper.

Scoop the meatball mixture into balls, each weighing about 2 ounces (56 g), and arrange on the prepared baking tray.

Wipe out the skillet and return it to medium heat. Add enough oil to just barely cover the bottom of the pan. Heat the oil briefly and, working in batches, add the meatballs, leaving about ½ inch (1 cm) between them. I like to flatten them lightly with the back of a spatula once they are in the pan, but you can make them round if you like. Decrease the heat to medium-low and fry until golden brown and cooked through, 6 to 8 minutes. Transfer the meatballs to an oven-safe dish and keep warm in the oven while you finish frying. Cook the remaining meatballs in the same fashion, adding more oil as necessary. Serve immediately with a bowl of the tarragon cream.

The cooked meatballs can be stored in the freezer for up to 1 month.

Oat and Sunflower Seed Cakes

with Herbed Yogurt

I first found a version of this recipe in a Danish food magazine, but over the ten-plus years I've been making it, it has morphed into my own. It's one of those go-to meals for when there isn't much in the kitchen other than some pantry basics—I almost always have eggs, oats, and yogurt on hand. The key to a light and fluffy cake is to whip the egg whites just before pan-frying. I like to serve the cakes with brown rice and a big leafy salad, but they're just as good on their own, in a lunch box, with a generous dollop of herbed yogurt. **MAKES 18 CAKES**

4 eggs, separated

1 tablespoon rye flour

2⁄3 cup (160 g) whole milk

2 cups (210 g) old-fashioned rolled oats

1 teaspoon madras curry powder

1 teaspoon kosher salt, plus more as needed

1⁄2 teaspoon ground turmeric

6 sprigs of flat-leaf parsley, leaves chopped

3⁄4 cup (112 g) toasted sunflower seeds (see Toasting Nuts and Seeds, page 42)

Freshly ground black pepper

Neutral oil, for frying

2 cups (500 g) Herbed Yogurt (page 60)

In a large bowl, stir together the egg yolks, rye flour, milk, oats, curry powder, salt, and turmeric. Set aside for 10 minutes while the oats soak up the milk. Stir in the parsley, sunflower seeds, and a few grinds of pepper.

In the bowl of a stand mixer fitted with the whisk attachment or in a large bowl with a whisk, whip the egg whites with a pinch of salt to soft peaks. Using a rubber spatula, fold half the egg whites into the oat mixture and, once incorporated, follow with the second half.

I always fry off a small sample before frying an entire batch of a mixture to make sure the seasonings are on point. Heat a medium skillet over medium heat, add a few drops of oil, and brown a tablespoon-size amount of the cake base on both sides, until cooked through, 1 to 2 minutes per side. Let cool slightly. Taste and add more salt or pepper to the main batch, if necessary. Fry off another sample, if necessary.

Return the skillet to medium heat. Add enough oil to just barely cover the bottom of the pan. Heat the oil briefly and, working in batches, scoop the batter into roughly 2-tablespoon-size mounds, placing them directly into the pan. (I love a spring-loaded scoop for this kind of job.) Fry until golden brown, 2 to 3 minutes per side. Transfer the cakes to an oven-safe dish. (It's a good idea to keep them warm in a 190°F / 90°C oven while you finish frying.) Cook the remaining cakes in the same fashion, adding more oil as necessary to encourage the formation of a nice crust. Serve immediately, accompanied by the herbed yogurt and a leafy green salad.

The cooked cakes and herbed yogurt can be stored separately in airtight containers in the refrigerator for 3 days and reheated in a 350°F (175°C) oven for about 10 minutes.

Green Egg Salad
with Pickled Red Onions

A twist on a classic, this egg salad is packed with fresh greens—peppery cress, chives, and parsley—but can just as easily be made with chopped broccoli, kale, or arugula. The stems get chopped and added to the salad, too—you would never notice them, and it means less food waste. When I make this at home, my teenage boys, who usually have strong opinions about green stuff, suddenly do not mind eating watercress.

Dr. Seuss may have preferred green eggs and ham, but I would rather have this version any day. Creamy, herby, and brightened with a hit of pickled red onions, I love to eat it for lunch, as served here, on a thick slice of rye bread, but sometimes, I'll just spoon it into a small bowl and use it as a dip for raw vegetable spears. **MAKES 2¾ CUPS**

- 6 hard-boiled eggs (see Perfect Hard-Boiled Eggs, page 154)
- 1 tablespoon minced shallot
- 3 tablespoons mayonnaise, preferably homemade
- 1 tablespoon sour cream
- 2 tablespoons Dijon mustard
- 1 cup (20 g) chopped watercress leaves and stems
- 1 bunch of chives, minced
- ½ cup (10 g) minced fresh flat-leaf parsley leaves and stems
- Kosher salt and freshly ground black pepper
- 6 to 8 (½-inch-thick) slices dark rye bread (or do thin slices, if you prefer!)
- 3 ounces (84 g) microgreens or sprouts, for serving
- Pickled Red Onions (page 48), for serving

Peel and finely chop the eggs. In a bowl, stir together the shallot, mayonnaise, sour cream, and mustard. Fold in the watercress, chives, and parsley, followed by the chopped eggs. Season with salt and pepper.

Serve with the bread, microgreens, and pickled onions.

The egg salad can be made in advance and stored in an airtight container in the refrigerator for up to 3 days.

perfect hard-boiled eggs

A boiled egg in its shell is a natural on-the-go food for lunch boxes, picnics, and hikes (when the urge for some outdoors-y Norwegian *friluft* strikes)! As much as boiling eggs seems straightforward, getting them right requires some attention.

At Kantine, we've boiled more eggs than I can count, whether for Green Egg Salad with Pickled Red Onions (page 153), a recipe inspired by all things green, or for our catered events where smoked trout deviled eggs are always a hit. (If you must know, the yolks are mixed with crème fraîche, Dijon mustard, finely flaked smoked trout, and plenty of fresh dill, then spooned back into the egg whites and topped with pearls of trout roe.)

To make hard-boiled eggs a bit fancy, peel them after cooling and let them sit overnight in the brine from Pickled Beets (page 48) to turn their exterior a gorgeous shade of pink.

To make perfect hard-boiled eggs, place 2 to 10 eggs in a pot and add cold water to cover by 1 inch (2.5 cm). Bring to a boil over high heat. As soon as the water comes to a full boil, decrease the heat to medium-high and immediately set a timer for 8 to 12 minutes, depending on your desired doneness (see Note for timing tips).

While the eggs cook, fill a large bowl with water and an ample amount of ice cubes. As soon as your timer goes off, use a slotted spoon to remove the eggs from the boiling water and transfer them to the ice bath. Don't skip this step, as the ice makes the shell and sticky membrane easier to peel off. Let them soak until they are cool to the touch, then peel to use or store in their shells in the refrigerator.

Note: For thoroughly hard-boiled eggs, cook them for 11 to 12 minutes. If you are hard-boiling 11 or more eggs, increase the cooking time to about 13 minutes. If you like a slightly creamy yolk, cook the eggs for 8 to 9 minutes.

Chanterelle, Charred Corn, and Goat Cheese Tartlets

These tartlets bring me back to the many ways we would use chanterelles when we struck gold in the Swedish woods near our summerhouse. Such a luxury! This isn't the kind of recipe you throw together in 30 minutes—the pastry is made like a quick puff pastry, though "quick" is relative when compared to the traditionally laminated pastry. But the effort is worth it, creating a beautifully flaky, herb-flecked base that pairs perfectly with the earthy chanterelles, sweet charred corn, and tangy goat cheese. Just make sure the butter stays very cold at every stage so the dough properly puffs in the oven. **MAKES 8 TARTLETS**

HERBED PASTRY CRUST

2¼ cups (288 g) all-purpose flour, plus more for rolling

½ teaspoon kosher salt

14 tablespoons (200 g) very cold unsalted butter

8 tablespoons (118 g) very cold water

2 tablespoons finely chopped fresh soft herbs (such as tarragon, thyme, chives, and/or parsley leaves), plus torn leaves for garnish

TOPPINGS AND ASSEMBLY

1 large ear of fresh corn, shucked

Extra-virgin olive oil

Kosher salt and freshly ground black pepper

1 tablespoon unsalted butter

8 ounces (224 g) fresh chanterelle or oyster mushrooms, or other mushrooms of your choice, thickly sliced (or halved if small)

4 ounces (112 g) fresh goat cheese

6 tablespoons (90 g) heavy cream, or as needed

1 egg, for egg wash

Make the crust. In a medium bowl, whisk together the flour and salt. Dice half the butter and toss it into the flour mixture until well combined. Thinly slice the remaining butter and add to the flour mixture. Use your hands to break up the butter into slightly smaller pieces and gently mix it into the flour. Sprinkle the water over the flour mixture, 1 tablespoon at a time, while tossing it together with your hands. Press the dough into a shaggy mass. It should clump together when pressed.

Dump the dough out onto a lightly floured work surface. With your hands, press the dough into a rectangle that is about ¾-inch (2 cm) thick. Fold the dough into thirds, like folding a letter, then gently flatten the rectangle and press it together into a slightly messy mass. Wrap the dough tightly in plastic wrap or parchment paper and refrigerate for at least 2 hours and up to overnight.

Remove the dough from the refrigerator; if it's very cold, let it rest for about 5 minutes.

On a lightly floured work surface, roll out the dough into a ½-inch (1 cm) thick rectangle, about 11 by 7 inches (28 by 18 cm), turning and flouring as you go to keep it from sticking. Sprinkle the herbs over the top of the dough, gently pressing them into the dough. Fold the dough into thirds, like folding a letter, then turn it clockwise and roll it out again into a ½-inch (1 cm) thick rectangle, again to about 11 by 7 inches (28 by 18 cm). Finally, fold it like a letter, turn it, roll it into a ½-inch (1 cm) thick rectangle, then fold it like a letter for a final time.

Wrap the dough tightly in plastic wrap or parchment paper and refrigerate for at least 30 minutes and up to overnight before using. (The dough can be frozen for up to 3 months at this point; thaw overnight in the refrigerator before using.)

CONTINUED

On a lightly floured work surface, roll out the dough into a ¼-inch (6 mm) thick rectangle. Trim the edges; the rectangle should measure approximately 14 by 10 inches (40 by 25 cm). Using a chef's knife or pizza cutter, cut the dough in half lengthwise to create two 14 by 5-inch (36 by 13 cm) strips. Then cut each strip crosswise into four pieces, each about 3½ inches (9 cm) wide by 5 inches (13 cm) tall. Line two large baking trays with parchment paper, then arrange four dough rectangles on each tray. Refrigerate while you prepare the toppings. Trimmings can be baked off for a crispy snack.

Prepare the toppings. Heat a large cast-iron skillet over medium-high heat. Break the ear of corn in half. Rub each half with a little olive oil, then season with salt. Sear the corn pieces, turning as needed, until some of the kernels have dark brown spots, 10 to 14 minutes. Transfer to a cutting board. When the corn is cool enough to handle, stand one of the ears vertically on its end in a medium bowl and, using a chef's knife, carefully cut the kernels off the cob.

Wipe out the skillet and return it to medium-high heat. Add the butter and, when melted, add the chanterelles. Season with salt and pepper. Cook, stirring occasionally, until just tender, about 4 minutes. Transfer to the bowl with the corn, toss to combine, and let cool completely.

In a bowl, stir together the goat cheese and enough cream to create a spreadable consistency.

Position two racks in the oven and preheat to 400°F (200°C).

Assemble. In a small bowl, beat together the egg with 1 teaspoon water to make an egg wash. Brush the egg wash over the top of the pastry rectangles. Using a paring knife, cut a border ½ inch (1 cm) from the edge of the pastry, cutting halfway through the pastry (be careful not to go all the way through). This shallow cut will create a border around the toppings when baked.

Divide the goat cheese mixture evenly among the pastry, using an offset spatula to spread it out, while leaving the border free from filling. Top each pastry with the mushroom-corn mixture, dividing it evenly and spreading it over the goat cheese mixture.

Bake until the pastry is crisp and golden brown, rotating the baking trays between the oven racks about halfway through, about 30 minutes total. Let cool for 10 minutes, then garnish with herbs and serve warm or at room temperature.

Trout and Cucumber Tartare

Normally, I veer away from farmed fish, opting for wild when it's in season. But here in Northern California, McFarland Springs trout is an exception. Sustainably raised and available year-round, it's served at many of the best restaurants in the area, and has been a staple at Kantine since the day we opened. (If you haven't read about their practices, I recommend looking them up—the work they do is truly impressive. The fish is also available in the Portland area.) At any given time, we use this trout in multiple menu items, especially our popular smoked trout salad. We've served this tartare at many events, and it's become a mainstay of our catering menu. It works beautifully atop cucumber disks, in little lettuce cups, on rye crackers, or simply in a bowl with crusty bread alongside—its presentation adapts easily to any format. **MAKES 4 SERVINGS**

In a medium bowl, combine the vinegar, shallot, dill, chives, mint, mustard, and a pinch of salt. Stir to combine. Add the trout, cucumber, and radish and stir gently to combine. Taste and season with salt as needed. Garnish with the roe, if using. Serve immediately in a small bowl accompanied by rye crackers and lettuce leaves, with lemon wedges for squeezing.

- 1 tablespoon golden or white balsamic vinegar
- 1 tablespoon minced shallot
- 2 teaspoons minced fresh dill
- 1 teaspoon minced fresh chives
- 1 teaspoon minced fresh mint
- ½ teaspoon Dijon mustard
- Kosher salt
- 12 ounces (336 g) sashimi-grade ocean (or sustainably raised) trout, skinned and trimmed, pin bones removed, and cut into ¼-inch (6 mm) dice (about 1 packed cup / 265 g once prepped)
- ¾ cup (120 g) peeled, halved, seeded, and diced ¼ inch (6mm) thick cucumber (preferably Persian or English)
- 1 radish, finely diced (about 2 tablespoons)
- 2 tablespoons trout roe (optional)
- Rye crackers and small lettuce leaves, such as Little Gem, for serving
- Lemon wedges, for serving

Vegetarian Mushroom Pâté

In Scandinavia, vegetarian pâtés come in many forms—some with a nut base, others with a legume base—but this rich, savory, and satisfying mushroom-based recipe is a favorite. I can never resist the deep umami of meaty mushrooms, enhanced by a touch of liquid aminos. Unlike the shelf-stable canned versions found in grocery and health food stores, this is a fresh, spreadable pâté, perfect for making an open-faced sandwich and pairing with a hearty salad for a simple meal, or adding to a snack board with crunchy crackers. The key to creating a smooth, spreadable texture is to chop the mushrooms finely. (If necessary, portobellos can replace the creminis, just make sure to use their de-stemmed weight before chopping.) **MAKES 1 "LOAF"**

PÂTÉ

Neutral oil, for greasing

2 tablespoons unsalted butter

4 tablespoons extra-virgin olive oil

1 pound (454 g) cremini mushrooms, brushed clean and finely chopped

5 ounces (140 g) shiitake mushrooms, stemmed, brushed clean, and finely chopped

1 teaspoon kosher salt, plus more as needed

Freshly ground black pepper

1 medium yellow onion, finely chopped

2 garlic cloves, minced

2 large sprigs of thyme, stemmed and leaves finely chopped

1 cup (140 g) toasted hazelnuts (see Toasting Nuts and Seeds, page 42)

1 cup (240 g) heavy cream

3 eggs

1 tablespoon liquid aminos

3 tablespoons all-purpose flour

¼ teaspoon ground allspice

FOR SERVING

6 to 8 thin slices dark rye bread

½ cup (100 g) Pickled Beets (page 48)

1 small cucumber, preferably Persian or English, sliced

3 ounces (84 g) microgreens or sprouts

Preheat the oven to 350°F (175°C). Lightly oil a 9 by 5-inch (23 by 13 cm) loaf pan. Line it with parchment paper so that the paper on the long sides hangs over by about 2 inches (5 cm).

In a large Dutch oven over medium-high heat, melt the butter with 2 tablespoons of the olive oil. Add all the mushrooms, season with salt and pepper, and cook, stirring occasionally, until soft and the liquid has been completely cooked off, about 8 minutes. Transfer to a medium bowl to cool.

Return the pan to medium heat and add the remaining 2 tablespoons olive oil. Add the onion, garlic, and thyme and cook, stirring occasionally, until the onion has softened and the mixture is fragrant, about 4 minutes.

In a blender, combine the onion mixture, hazelnuts, cream, eggs, liquid aminos, flour, allspice, 1 teaspoon of the salt, and a few grinds of pepper. Blend until homogeneous. Pour this mixture over the mushrooms and stir to combine.

Pour the mixture into the prepared loaf pan and bake until firm and slightly puffed in the center, about 1 hour. Transfer to a rack to cool. Serve warm or room temperature, still in the pan. Enjoy a thick slathering on the rye bread with the pickled beets, cucumbers, and microgreens alongside.

discovering swedish sandwich cake

At Kantine, we receive a good number of specialty bakery orders, especially for cakes. A few years back we got a request from someone looking to order a *smörgåstårta*, or Swedish sandwich cake, for their child's baptism. To be honest, I'd never heard of the cake prior to then, and it got me wondering why this cake had never appeared on my radar during the fifteen years I lived literally right next to Sweden, and how on earth my Swedish friends living in Denmark had successfully hidden this piece of Swedish food culture from me.

Curious, I went online to do research. When the first images popped up, I was genuinely surprised: There they were, cakes of all shapes and sizes, elaborately garnished and colorful. When I looked closer, I discovered what makes this cake unique: It's a savory cake meant to be served as a meal! Instead of sweet cake layers, it has layers of crustless white bread, the fillings and spreads are savory, and the exterior "frosting" is simply cream cheese and sour cream or whipped heavy cream topped with garnishes of hard-boiled egg wedges, sprigs of dill, pearls of fish roe, asparagus spears, strips of cucumber, and gravlax or ham rosettes.

The photos of this culinary trompe l'oeil fascinated me, and I fell immediately into a deep rabbit hole. As it turns out, sandwich cakes aren't anything new—they've been around since the 1930s—but it wasn't until about a decade later that they began to resemble the ornately decorated cakes of today. Back then, sandwich cakes were the perfect dish to serve guests at home or at special gatherings like funerals or christenings because they required a lot less work than a multicourse meal and could be made a day or two in advance, allowing hosts time to be more attentive to their guests.

In the 1960s, Swedish confectioner Gunnar Sjödahl began making sandwich cakes, and to this day, he is regarded by many as the true creator of the modern-day version, which has multiple layers, more refined fillings, and elaborate decorations. During his culinary career, Gunnar reportedly made hundreds of thousands of cakes, and in fact, Gunnar's birthday—November 13—is now known in Sweden as Sandwich Cake Day (*Smörgåstårtans Dag*) to honor his contribution.

Although the sandwich cake's popularity in urban areas faded during the 1980s and '90s, it was anything but forgotten in Sweden's countryside, where grocery stores to this day stock finished cakes as well as precut frozen crustless white bread for those who wanted to make one at home.

The endless ways a sandwich cake can be customized has allowed it to remain relevant throughout time. You can add or subtract ingredients to suit your liking, and there are very few rules to follow. Many years ago, cake fillings were made with ground beef, liver pâté, and *mimosasallad* (a curious fruit salad dressed with mayonnaise and Dijon!), whereas today's smörgåstårta features more fresh and vibrant ingredients, with less meat and more vegetables.

A few years back, we created an Easter lunch bundle as a pickup grab bag at Kantine, and sandwich cakes were one of the main food items in the bundle. Once word got out about what we were offering, the bundle sold out immediately. Needless to say, my kitchen staff and I got plenty of practice baking white sandwich bread, making fillings, and assembling, frosting, and garnishing the cakes. As soon as the last order was out the door, I made one more cake—this time just for my family—creating a truly memorable Easter meal.

tips for swedish sandwich cake

Smörgåstårta is meant to be as beautiful as it is delicious. Here are a few cake tips that even Swedish confectioner Gunnar Sjödahl (see page 162) would likely have approved.

Use good bread.

The foundation of a great smörgåstårta is the bread, so if you aren't planning on baking the Malted Sandwich Bread (page 233), choose something soft but sturdy. A homemade loaf or a high-quality store-bought white or pain de mie works best. I've seen some cakes made with dark rye bread, too!

Be generous with the filling.

A sandwich cake is all about multiple bread layers, and skimpy fillings make for a dry and boring bite. The moisture from the fillings is meant to soak slightly into the bread, giving it the right texture without making it soggy.

Contrast flavors and textures.

A good smörgåstårta has balance: something creamy, something fresh, something with a little tang or bite. Think creamy seafood salad with crisp cucumbers, or smoked ham with a punchy mustard spread.

Make your cake a day ahead.

Smörgåstårta tastes best when it's had time to chill (wrapped well) in the refrigerator, preferably overnight, so the bread can soak up the moisture from the fillings and frosting and the flavors can meld together.

Keep the garnishes elegant, simple, and fresh.

Have a general idea of what your finished cake should look like and don't overdo it. Thinly sliced radishes, sprigs of fresh herbs, microgreens, poppy seeds, and delicate rosettes of smoked salmon or ham add just enough detail to make the cake eye-catching but not over-the-top. Gather inspiration online.

Smörgåstårta

(Swedish Sandwich Cake)

Here's your chance to re-create a Swedish classic at home. With layers of seafood and egg salads, dense bread, and a creamy spread, smörgåstårta is far more filling than it looks. You can follow this recipe—my go-to—or make your own version (see Tips for Swedish Sandwich Cake, page 164). Just be sure the fillings are creamy and generous—ask any Swede, they'll tell you there's nothing worse than a dry smörgåstårta.

Decorate the frosted cake with toppings that mirror the fillings. In this case, smoked trout, bay shrimp, fresh dill and chives, and hard-boiled eggs would all be fitting. For a touch of freshness and color, add other garnishes like blanched asparagus spears, watercress, edible flowers, sprouts, or thinly sliced radishes. However you assemble it, this is a dish that's bound to impress. **MAKES ONE 8-INCH (20 CM) ROUND CAKE**

TROUT FILLING

- 3 ounces (84 g) smoked trout, flaked, plus more for decorating
- 3 hard-boiled eggs (see Perfect Hard-Boiled Eggs, page 154), peeled and finely chopped, plus more for decorating
- ¼ cup (63 g) sour cream
- 2 tablespoons chopped fresh chives, plus more for decorating
- Kosher salt and freshly ground black pepper

SHRIMP FILLING

- 1 cup (195 g) cooked pink bay shrimp, plus more for decorating
- ⅓ cup (65 g) mayonnaise
- ¼ cup (63 g) sour cream
- 2 tablespoons chopped fresh dill, plus sprigs for decorating
- 2 teaspoons peeled and finely grated fresh horseradish
- ½ teaspoon Dijon mustard
- 1 teaspoon fresh lemon juice, or as needed
- Kosher salt and freshly ground black pepper

THE "FROSTING"

- 8 ounces (227 g) cream cheese, cut into chunks, at room temperature
- ¾ cup (189 g) sour cream
- Kosher salt and freshly ground black pepper

ASSEMBLY

- Malted Sandwich Bread (page 233), baked as an 8-inch (20 cm) round (see Tips for Swedish Sandwich Cake, page 164), or a high-quality store-bought white bread or pain de mie with crusts cut off

Make the trout filling. In a medium bowl, gently stir together the trout, eggs, sour cream, and chives. Season with salt and pepper. Refrigerate until ready to use.

Make the shrimp filling. In a medium bowl, gently stir together the shrimp, mayonnaise, sour cream, dill, horseradish, and mustard. Stir in the lemon juice, then season with salt and pepper. Refrigerate until ready to use.

Make the "frosting." In the bowl of a stand mixer fitted with the paddle attachment, beat the cream cheese and sour cream until very smooth, 2 to 3 minutes. Season with salt and pepper.

Assemble the sandwich cake. Cut the crusts off the top and sides of the bread. Slice it horizontally twice to create three equal layers. Place the bottom slice on a platter, then spread with the trout filling. Top with the middle bread layer and spread with the shrimp filling. Place the top third bread layer on top of the shrimp filling.

Once your cake is layered up, spread the "frosting" over the whole smörgåtårta. As with icing a sweet layer cake, it's easiest to use an offset spatula and spread one thin layer over everything first to seal in the crumbs and then go back and apply a thicker layer. Cover the sandwich cake loosely with plastic wrap or a plastic bag and refrigerate overnight for best results.

Just before serving, decorate the cake (see headnote). Transfer the cake to a serving platter and present the unsliced cake to your amazed guests before cutting into thin slices.

SOUP'S ON

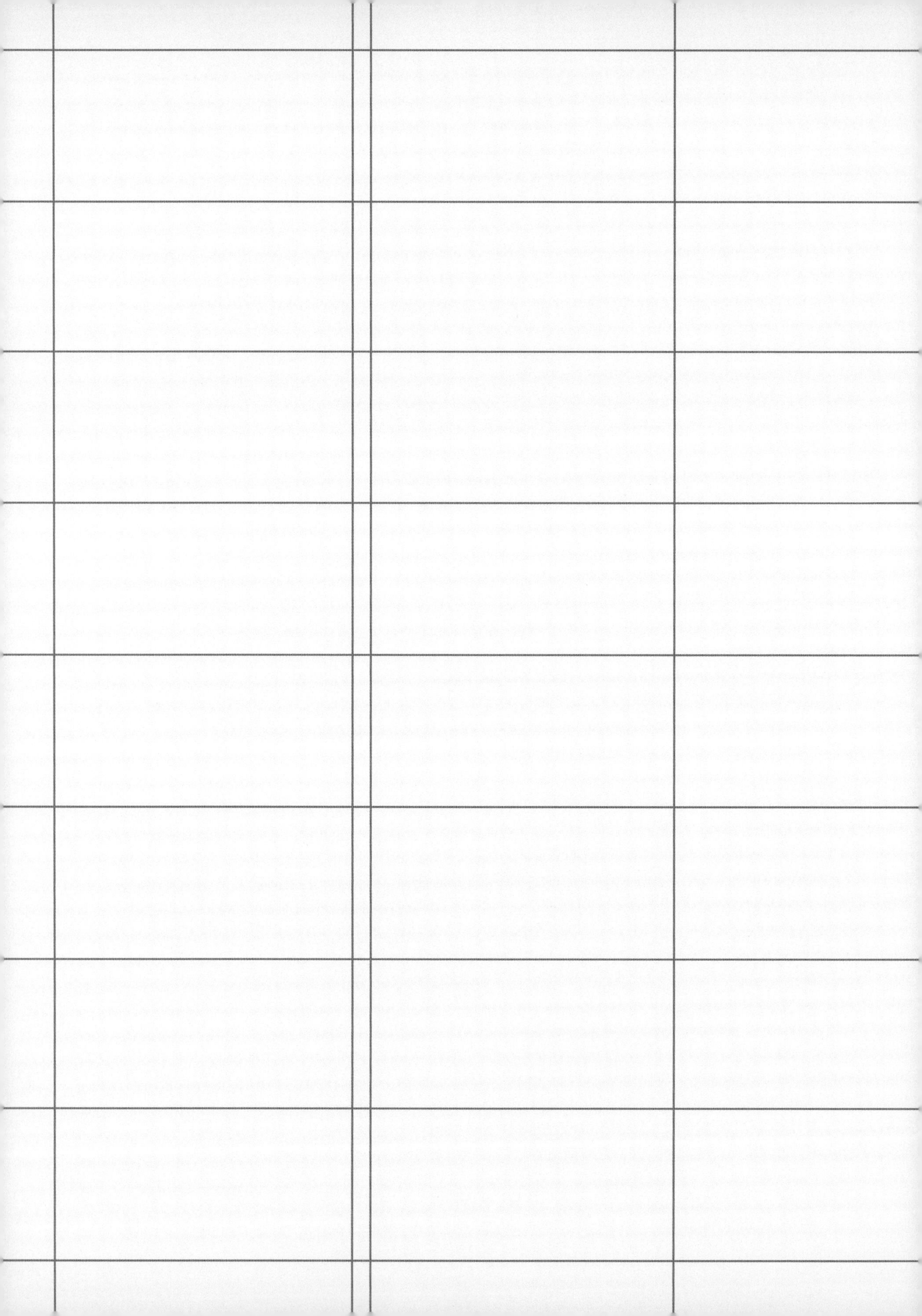

My good friend Paula grew up in Vallentuna, a suburb of Stockholm, and when she was a child, every Thursday, without fail, Paula's mother would do the same thing most Swedes were doing: make pea soup (*ärtsoppa*) for dinner. Just as Paula's school week started on Monday and the weekend began on Friday, pea soup was always, always eaten on Thursdays. Paula and her parents ate the thick soup piping hot, with a spoonful of mustard on top. And after the soup? Pancakes, of course. Thin and crepe-like, served with *drottningsylt* (a jam of blueberries and raspberries) and whipped cream. Paula never questioned the soup and pancake tradition. It was just what Swedes did.

Yellow pea soup and pancakes on Thursdays is a tradition that stretches back to the 1700s and has become woven into Swedish food culture. Some say the practice began as a way to prepare Catholics for fasting on Fridays. Others say it came from the Swedish military, who long served pea soup on Thursdays because it was hearty, inexpensive, and easy to cook in bulk. (To this day, you can buy "Soldier's Pea Soup" in a can, and according to Paula, it's the next best thing to homemade.) Either way, the soup tradition has endured, and you'll still find Swedish Yellow Pea Soup (page 173) served in restaurants, school cafeterias, and homes across Sweden each and every Thursday.

While Sweden may have the most well-known soup tradition in Scandinavia, soups of all kinds have long been a practical, comforting, and necessary food across the region. Winters are dark and long, and a steaming bowl of something rich and robust—Lentil Spinach Soup (page 184) or Cauliflower Soup with Golden Garlic and Toasted Seeds (page 188)—is often the only thing that makes sense on a frigid night. Soups that thaw you from the inside out.

But soup in Scandinavia isn't just about winter survival. It shifts with the seasons, too. During Danish summertime, chilled soups like Red Fruit Soup (page 259) or buttermilk soup (*koldskål*) keep us cool when hot food is just too, eh, hot.

Soup is also deeply tied to the Scandinavian concept of togetherness. It's usually shared with others, served from a heavy-bottomed enameled pot in the middle of the table, with crusty bread to mop up the last bits. A pot of Salmon and Roasted Corn Chowder (page 181) in Norway marks the wild salmon season, while a cup of Spiced Tomato Soup with Barley (page 177) is the perfect vessel for dunking a grilled Havarti cheese and rye bread sandwich.

There's a reason soup remains a staple in schools, workplaces, and homes—it is nourishing, filling, and naturally communal. Soup haters, beware. This chapter might just change your mind.

Swedish Yellow Pea Soup

In Sweden, *ärtsoppa*—pea soup—is traditionally eaten on Thursdays, often followed by pancakes for dessert. While sweet pancakes are the classic pairing, I prefer serving the soup with something savory to dip in the soup instead (see Thursday's Savory Oat Pancakes, page 243). The soup is simple but deeply flavorful, made with yellow peas and a smoky ham hock. If you can't find a smoked pork shank, a turkey wing or smoked pork belly (10 ounces) works just as well. Of course, the soup can be made vegetarian by omitting the meat (and the second saucepan) entirely, and just using a flavorful vegetable stock in place of the meat broth.

Yellow or green split peas will do, but if you want to make it truly authentic, whole yellow peas can be found online. Rutabaga adds an earthy sweetness, but potatoes, sweet potatoes, or even golden beets make good substitutes. To serve, a small bowl of grainy mustard on the side is a must. And if you want to lean even more into tradition, do as many Swedes do and pair your soup with a glass of warm *punsch*, a sweet and bitter spiced liqueur. **MAKES 8 SERVINGS**

3 cups (600 g) dried whole yellow peas, soaked overnight at room temperature

2 bay leaves

4 whole cloves

3 sprigs of thyme

2 small yellow onions, one halved, one finely diced (11 ounces / 300 g)

2 pounds (907 g) smoked pork or ham shank

Kosher salt and freshly ground black pepper

1 small celery root, peeled and finely diced (about 1½ cups / 176 g)

3 medium carrots, scrubbed and finely diced (about 1½ cups / 210 g)

1 medium rutabaga, peeled and finely diced (about 1½ cups / 210 g)

Leaves from ½ bunch of flat-leaf parsley, chopped

Grainy mustard, for serving

Crusty bread or Thursday's Savory Oat Pancakes, for serving

Drain the peas and transfer them to a large saucepan or Dutch oven. Add water to cover by a few inches, then add the bay leaves, cloves, thyme, and one half of the halved onion. Bring to a boil over high heat. Decrease the heat to medium-low and simmer, stirring occasionally and adding additional water if necessary, until the peas are soft without falling apart, 2 to 2½ hours. While they cook, skim and discard any foam that collects on the surface.

Meanwhile, add the shank to a separate large saucepan or Dutch oven and add water to cover by 2 inches (5 cm). Add the other half of the onion and a healthy pinch of salt. Bring to a boil over high heat. Decrease the heat to low and simmer, skimming and discarding any impurities that come to the surface, until the meat is tender and releases from the bone, about 3 hours.

Remove and discard the bay leaves, cloves, thyme, and half onion from the peas. I like to partially puree the soup, so it has both whole and blended peas. To do so, use an immersion blender to give the yellow peas a good blitz, leaving about half of the peas whole. Add the diced onion, celery root, carrots, and rutabaga to the pot and stir to combine. Add a bit of water or some of the cooking liquid from the meat to keep the peas from burning on the bottom of the pot. Partially cover the pot and cook over medium heat, stirring occasionally, until the vegetables are very tender, about 45 minutes. (Decrease the heat to medium-low or low if the soup starts to stick to the bottom.)

CONTINUED

When the meat is tender, remove the shank from the pot and let it cool for 15 minutes. Discard the bones and gristle and shred the meat by hand or with two forks. Add the meat to the soup and use some of the remaining cooking liquid to adjust the consistency, if necessary. (Be sure to skim the fat off the surface of the liquid with a ladle or large spoon first.) Season with salt and pepper.

When everything is tender, stir in the parsley and a few grinds of black pepper. Ladle the soup into bowls and serve with grainy mustard, which, depending on your style, can either be stirred into your bowl or left at the outside edge to be nipped at with each full spoonful of soup. Serve with crusty bread or savory oatmeal pancakes.

To store, let the soup cool to room temperature. Store in airtight containers in the refrigerator for up to 1 week or in the freezer for up to 1 month.

well seasoned

adding oomph with more than just salt

Years ago in Copenhagen, I worked as a chef at a preschool, and every day the principal would come in the kitchen around lunchtime to plate her lunch brought from home. She'd usually begin by laying a few slices of seedy rye bread on a plate, topping them with pork liver pâté, pickled beets, a handful of fresh sprouts, and a few grinds of black pepper. Alongside that, she'd assemble a small bowl of berries and toasted nuts. Her lunch always struck me as so well balanced, not just with a variety of food types but of textures and flavors: the richness of the pâté, the acidity of the pickled beets, the crisp freshness of the sprouts, and the sweetness and crunch of the berries and nuts. It was a perfect example of how thoughtful combinations—and not large portions—can become a meal that satiates and satisfies both hunger and the senses.

When it comes to enhancing flavor, salt can often single-handedly transform food from good to great. But even with an appropriate amount of salt, a dish still might seem to be lacking something. In those instances, I employ a few tricks of the trade to help ingredients work together to improve depth, balance, and/or flavor.

Here are six ways to enhance your food:

Use acid for brightness and to balance richness. Lemon juice, vinegar, or even a spoonful of pickle brine can lift a dish that tastes flat.

Add umami for depth. Umami is the savory quality that adds complexity to a dish. It can be found in ingredients like miso, soy sauce, tomatoes, mushrooms, nutritional yeast, or aged cheese like Parmesan. Adding just a small amount works wonders.

Call on kokumi. *Kokumi* is a Japanese term for an enhanced and lingering mouthfeel, so it's not a flavor per se, but a characteristic that comes into play when refining the quality of a dish. Ingredients like slow-cooked broths, caramelized onions, roasted garlic, and fermented foods all possess kokumi, and when utilized, they add fullness and depth, which leads to a more satisfying flavor.

Throw in a little sweetness. A pinch of sugar, honey, or maple syrup can round out acidity and bitterness, making flavors feel more in harmony. I remind myself of this tip particularly often when I am making vinaigrettes or Spiced Tomato Soup with Barley (page 177).

Finish with fresh herbs. Robust herbs like thyme and rosemary do well when added at the beginning of cooking, but don't forget about the beauty of soft herbs like parsley, basil, chives, and dill. Sprinkling them into your food near the end of cooking adds a fresh flavor and irresistible aroma.

Add texture. The addition of nuts, seeds, croutons, or even fried shallots to a dish undoubtedly brings in more flavor, and sometimes it's just as much about the crunch. That textural contrast breaks up the monotony of softer foods and inevitably creates a more dynamic dish.

Spiced Tomato Soup with Barley

Many years ago, while working as a chef at a Danish preschool, I came across a tomato soup recipe by my now-friend Katrine Klinken, a Denmark-based chef, author, and food educator. Because the soup was pureed, it was a brilliant way to sneak in leftover vegetables and grains—no child was the wiser—and in fact, they loved it. Over the years, I've adapted and added to Katrine's original, creating a version that's now one of my son's favorite foods (especially with a grilled cheese sandwich). The soup is dairy-free, and with the addition of barley, a big bowl makes for a satisfying and filling lunch.

MAKES 4 TO 6 SERVINGS

½ cup (100 g) pearled barley

1½ cups (360 g) water

SOUP

3 tablespoons neutral oil

1 medium onion (6 ounces / 168 g), sliced

1 tablespoon peeled and minced ginger

2 garlic cloves, minced

2 medium green peppers (13½ ounces / 380 g), seeded and chopped

1½ tablespoons madras curry powder

28 ounces (794 g) canned crushed tomatoes

11 ounces (300 g) coconut milk

2 teaspoons kosher salt, plus more as needed

Freshly ground black pepper

Brown sugar or balsamic vinegar, as needed

Extra-virgin olive oil, for serving

1 bunch of chives, cut into ½-inch (1 cm) pieces, for serving

In a small saucepan, combine the barley and water. Add a pinch of salt and bring to a boil. Skim and discard any foam that collects on the surface. Once boiling, decrease the heat to low, cover, and cook until the barley is tender and chewy, about 25 minutes, adding a bit more water if necessary. Drain the barley in a colander, if necessary, and then pour the barley out onto a baking tray to cool. The barley can be made in advance and stored in a freezer bag or an airtight container in the refrigerator for up to 5 days or in the freezer for up to 3 months.

Make the soup. Heat a large Dutch oven over medium heat. Add the oil, followed by the onion, ginger, and garlic. Cook, stirring often, until tender but not yet browning, 3 to 4 minutes. Decrease the heat to medium-low and add the green peppers. Cook until the onions are golden brown and the green peppers are slightly soft, about 5 minutes. Add the curry powder and cook until fragrant, 1 minute. Add the tomatoes and rinse the can with 1 cup (240 g) water, then add that to the pot as well. Add 1 to 1½ cups (4 to 6½ ounces / 120 to 180 g) cooked vegetables and/or grains if you have leftovers hanging around (see headnote), but if not, proceed without. Give everything a good stir and then put a lid on it. Decrease the heat to low and simmer for 15 minutes, stirring occasionally.

Remove the pot from the heat and, using an immersion blender (preferred), countertop blender, or food processor, puree the soup completely. Add the coconut milk to the pureed soup and bring it to a simmer over low heat, making sure not to let the soup come to a full boil. Season with the salt and pepper. If the soup needs a touch of sweetness for balance, add a teaspoon of brown sugar or balsamic vinegar. Ladle into shallow bowls and top with spoonfuls of the cooked barley, a swirl of olive oil, a bit of pepper, and a sprinkle of chives.

The soup can be made in advance (hold the barley separately) and stored in an airtight container in the refrigerator for up to 5 days. It's best to freeze the soup base, minus the coconut milk (it tends to turn grainy when frozen) and barley. The soup can be frozen for 2 to 3 months, and once thawed, the coconut milk and barley can be added.

Lemony Chickpea and Green Split Pea Stew

I grew up eating my mom's German green split pea soup, and while this version is quite different from that, it's the kind of soup I imagine the two of us would have enjoyed eating together. The leeks add a silky fullness to this soup, and if you've never cooked with them before, be sure to wash them well since their many layers tend to hide dirt and sand. Like many soups, I find that this one tastes even better the day after it's made, when flavors have melded and deepened—so much so that you might want to consider making a double batch. **MAKES 4 TO 6 SERVINGS**

2 tablespoons quinoa

1 medium leek, white and pale green parts only (27 ounces / 200 g)

SOUP

2 tablespoons neutral oil, or as needed

3 medium onions (18 ounces / 510 g), finely diced

5 garlic cloves, minced

½ large celery root (8 ounces / 224 g), peeled and cut into ½-inch (1 cm) dice

2 tablespoons Preserved Spent Lemon (page 59), rinsed and minced

¾ cup (150 g) dried green split peas, rinsed

6 cups (1.4 kg) low-sodium vegetable stock

29 ounces (812 g / about three 15-ounce cans) cooked or drained canned chickpeas

Kosher salt and freshly ground black pepper

1 teaspoon liquid aminos

Fresh lemon juice, as needed

1 cup (40 g) firmly packed baby spinach, for serving

½ cup (125 g) plain skyr or Greek yogurt, for serving

Heat a medium heavy-bottomed skillet over medium-high heat for 2 to 3 minutes. Pour the dry quinoa into the hot skillet and gently swirl for even heating. The quinoa will start to brown and puff after a few seconds. Continue to swirl and, when most of the quinoa has puffed, pour it immediately into a small bowl. (While you're at it, make a double batch to have on hand in your pantry—puffed quinoa adds a great crunch to salads, smoothies, and granola. Be sure to keep your batches small to ensure best results.)

Halve the leek lengthwise, then cut crosswise into 1-inch (2.5 cm) pieces. Add to a large bowl half full of water and swirl them around and separate the layers to remove any dirt. The leek will float, and the dirt should sink to the bottom of the bowl.

Make the soup. In a large Dutch oven over medium heat, heat the oil. Add the onions, garlic, and celery root. Using your hands, remove the leeks from the water and add them to the saucepan (you want some residual water to help sweat the leeks). Cook, stirring occasionally, until the mixture is tender without coloring, 5 to 7 minutes. Add the preserved lemon and split peas and cook for another 2 to 3 minutes while stirring.

Add the stock and bring it to a simmer. Decrease the heat to low and simmer uncovered until the split peas are cooked through, about 15 minutes. Add the chickpeas and bring back to a simmer. Remove the pot from the heat and, using an immersion blender (preferred), countertop blender, or food processor, puree approximately half of the soup to a chunky consistency, combining both halves afterward (if needed). Season with salt, pepper, the liquid aminos, and lemon juice.

When ready to serve, heat the soup thoroughly and, at the last minute, stir in the spinach (you just want to wilt it). Ladle into shallow bowls and finish with a spoonful of skyr and a sprinkle of the puffed quinoa.

The soup can be made in advance (hold the spinach for reheating) and stored in an airtight container in the refrigerator for up to 5 days. The soup base, minus the spinach (and skyr and quinoa), can be stored in the freezer for 2 to 3 months. Once thawed, stir in the fresh spinach and garnish with skyr and quinoa.

Salmon and Roasted Corn Chowder

This chowder is all about layers of smoky, sweet, and savory flavors. The combination of bacon, smoked salmon, and seared corn brings a deep richness, while fresh horseradish and dill add brightness.

Simmering the spent corn cobs in the soup reminds me of a restaurant I used to work at, where we'd regularly make corn broth as a flavorful vegetarian base. Here, it boosts the sweetness of the corn, which pairs so elegantly with the salmon. A bowl of this, with crusty bread to sop up the last bits, is my idea of comfort.

I have yet to meet a Norwegian whose eyes don't light up when I bring up the topic of salmon. In Norway, the arrival of wild salmon is treated with near reverence, so much so that in 2012, a twenty-four-hour "slow TV" live broadcast called *Salmon River—Minute by Minute* aired to mark the opening of the salmon season. Over one million viewers tuned in to watch fishermen cast lines into the Gaula River, to try their luck at bringing home this beloved fish. While this recipe may not be traditional, I imagine very few Norwegians would snub a bowl of it. **MAKES 6 SERVINGS**

2 large ears of fresh corn, shucked and broken in half crosswise

Neutral oil

3 slices (3 ounces / 84 g) thick-cut applewood-smoked bacon, chopped

½ medium yellow onion (3 ounces / 84 g), finely chopped

2 tablespoons unsalted butter

1 medium leek, white and pale green parts only (7 ounces / 200 g), quartered lengthwise and cut crosswise into ¼-inch (6 mm) slices

Kosher salt and freshly ground black pepper

2 tablespoons all-purpose flour

1 cup (240 g) dry white wine

2½ cups (600 g) low-sodium vegetable or chicken broth, plus more as needed

1 pound (450 g) yellow or Yukon gold potatoes, unpeeled, cut into ½-inch (1 cm) chunks

Heat a large Dutch oven over high heat. Rub the ears of corn lightly with oil, then add the corn to the pot and sear, turning occasionally, until browned in spots and crisp-tender, 5 to 8 minutes. Transfer the corn cobs to a cutting board. When cool enough to handle, stand one of the ears vertically on its end in a medium bowl and using a chef's knife, carefully cut the kernels off the cob. Repeat with the second ear of corn in the same bowl. You should have about 2 cups. Reserve the cobs.

Wipe out the Dutch oven if necessary, place it over medium-low heat, add the bacon, and cook until crisp, about 6 minutes. Using a slotted spoon, transfer to paper towels to drain. Pour off all but 1 tablespoon of the fat.

Increase the heat to medium and add the onion. Cook, stirring and scraping up any browned bits, until softened, about 4 minutes. Add the butter and leek and season with salt. Cook, stirring, until tender, about 4 minutes. Add the flour and stir until evenly moistened, then cook, stirring, for 1 minute to cook off the floury taste. While stirring constantly, slowly add the wine, scraping up any browned bits on the bottom of the pot, until the mixture thickens, about 2 minutes. Stir in the broth and 2 teaspoons salt, then add the potatoes and the cobs to the pot. Bring to a gentle boil over medium-high heat, then decrease the heat to medium-low, partially cover, and simmer until the potatoes are tender, about 20 minutes.

CONTINUED

2 pounds (900 g) fresh salmon fillets, skinned and pin bones removed, cut into 1-inch (2.5 cm) chunks

4 ounces (115 g) hot-smoked salmon, skinned and broken into bite-size chunks

½ cup (120 g) heavy cream, plus more as needed

½ cup (120 g) whole milk, plus more as needed

1 tablespoon peeled and finely grated fresh horseradish, plus more as needed

1 small bunch of chives, chopped

1 small bunch of dill, fronds and stems chopped

Crusty bread, for serving

Hold one of the reserved corn cobs over the pot and, using a butter knife, scrape each cob to remove the "milk." Repeat with the remaining cobs. Add the fresh and smoked salmon, reserved corn kernels, bacon, ½ cup of the cream, ½ cup of the milk, and 1 tablespoon of the grated horseradish to the pot and stir to combine. Add more horseradish if you'd like more of a kick. (If the mixture is too thick, add more cream, milk, or broth to achieve the consistency you desire.)

Simmer gently until the salmon is opaque and the soup is warmed through, about 4 minutes. Taste and adjust the seasoning with salt and pepper. Ladle into bowls, garnish with the chives and dill, and serve immediately with crusty bread.

The soup tastes best as soon as it's made, but it can be made in advance and stored in an airtight container in the refrigerator for up to 3 days. I don't recommend freezing this soup.

tips for freezing and reheating soups

Freezing soup is such a great way to ensure you always have something good to eat on hand. During the weekend, we often have leftover soup for lunch, paired with some crusty bread, and it never disappoints. Through trial and error, I've figured out quite a few dos and don'ts about freezing soup. Here are my "hot" tips for keeping your frozen soup stash at its absolute best.

Always leave room at the top of the container. Soup expands as it freezes, and if you fill the container to the brim, you risk a cracked lid or finding a uniquely flavored ice cube in the freezer. If you are using freezer bags, try to press out any air before sealing the bag.

In smaller households, **freeze soup in smaller portions,** preferably in silicone muffin tins. Once solid, unmold and transfer them to a bag or container. This way, you can thaw only as much as you need.

Broth-based soups freeze best, and I avoid freezing soups with dairy. Cream and milk don't freeze well and can get grainy when reheated. If a soup you want to freeze calls for dairy, wait to add it until after the soup base has been reheated.

Soups with grains or pasta tend to balloon up and get mushy after having been frozen. If possible, **cook and freeze the soup separately, and add the grains or pasta when reheating.**

Reheat your frozen soup slowly. Going straight from frozen to high heat can cause scorching on the bottom of your pot, as well as make the ingredients break down. If time allows, let soups thaw in the fridge overnight before reheating.

Lentil Spinach Soup

To celebrate my first New Year's Eve in Denmark, a few friends and I rented a Boy Scout camp just outside Copenhagen. We imagined hosting a cozy gathering with maybe twenty guests. But in the days leading up to the big night, word spread like wildfire, friends told friends, and our little party snowballed to a whopping sixty-five guests. With the promise of a multicourse meal to prepare, there was plenty of cooking to be done! That's when I decided that, in the middle of the woods on a chilly December evening, this hearty soup would make a fantastic first course.

Granted, it might not be the most breathtakingly beautiful soup, but it makes up for it in flavor—and that night, with the lights dimmed in the main cabin, no one noticed its understated appearance anyway. You can try other greens in place of the spinach—kale works well, and I've made a version with stinging nettles that has a lovely peppery edge (see A Forager at Heart, page 239). No need to be precise when chopping the vegetables, since they will be pureed anyway. A crumble of feta and a drizzle of good olive oil make the perfect finishing touch.

MAKES 4 TO 6 SERVINGS

- 3 tablespoons neutral oil
- 2 medium onions (12 ounces / 336 g), finely chopped
- 2 medium carrots (5 ounces / 140 g), scrubbed and finely chopped
- ¾ small celery root (about 4½ ounces / 126 g), peeled and finely chopped
- 1 teaspoon minced garlic
- 1¼ cups (250 g) green lentils
- 4½ cups (1.1 kg) low-sodium vegetable broth, plus more as needed
- Kosher salt and freshly ground black pepper
- 12 ounces (336 g) baby spinach
- 1 teaspoon white or apple cider vinegar
- Extra-virgin olive oil, for garnish
- 6 ounces (168 g) crumbled sheep's milk feta cheese (optional)

In a large Dutch oven over medium heat, heat 2 tablespoons of the neutral oil. Add the onions, carrots, celery root, and garlic and cook, stirring often, until tender and fragrant without color, about 10 minutes. Add the lentils and broth. Season generously with salt and a few grinds of pepper. Increase the heat to medium-high, bring to a gentle boil, then decrease the heat to medium-low and simmer gently, stirring occasionally, until the lentils are tender, 20 to 25 minutes.

Meanwhile, in a medium skillet over medium heat, warm the remaining 1 tablespoon of the neutral oil. Add the spinach and, using tongs, stir and turn the spinach until it just begins to wilt. Transfer to a small bowl and let cool.

Pour the lentil soup through a medium-mesh sieve, reserving the broth. Place the soup solids and spinach together in a food processor and pulse to a chunky puree. Return the puree to the Dutch oven. Add enough of the reserved broth to achieve a chunky consistency or the consistency you desire. Reheat the soup over medium heat, add the vinegar, and give it a final season with salt and pepper before ladling it into shallow bowls. Garnish with a drizzle of olive oil and the feta and serve at once.

The soup can be made in advance and stored in an airtight container in the refrigerator for up to 5 days. The soup base (minus the feta garnish) can be stored in the freezer for 2 to 3 months.

Sven's Meatball Soup

Sven, a German carpenter who'd lived in Denmark for most of his adult life, and I met when he came to my home to help me get started on a kitchen remodel. Soon we began talking about food, and before I knew it, he was staying for dinner with my family after his workday wrapped up. One day, after our old range was hauled and the new one hadn't yet arrived, Sven showed up with a hot plate and a pot of this hearty soup, and dinner that evening was saved. I've made this soup many times since, though one time I made it with an IPA, and the bitterness practically ruined it. Lesson learned, Sven was right: Lager is the only way to go. **MAKES 4 TO 6 SERVINGS**

2 tablespoons neutral oil, plus more as needed

2 tablespoons unsalted butter

1½ medium yellow onions (9 ounces / 252 g), diced

2 small carrots (4 ounces / 112 g), scrubbed and cut into ½-inch (1 cm) dice

2 celery stalks (4 ounces / 112 g), cut into ½-inch (1 cm) dice

1 teaspoon peeled and minced ginger

A few gratings of nutmeg

2 tablespoons rye flour

10 ounces (280 g) creamer potatoes, cut into 1-inch (2.5 cm) pieces

7 ounces (200 g) butternut squash, peeled and cut into 1-inch (2.5 cm) pieces

2 teaspoons Dijon mustard

12 ounces (336 g) lager (such as Heineken or Grolsch)

3 cups (720 g) low-sodium chicken or vegetable broth, plus more as needed

5 ounces (140 g) egg noodles

¼ cup (63 g) sour cream

Kosher salt and freshly ground black pepper

20 to 24 fully cooked Scandinavian Meatballs (page 194, about half the recipe)

5 sprigs of flat-leaf parsley, leaves chopped

In a large Dutch oven over medium heat, heat the oil and butter. When the butter has melted, add the onions, carrots, celery, and ginger. Cook, stirring occasionally, until tender without coloring, 5 to 7 minutes. Add the nutmeg and flour and stir until well combined, then cook for another 2 minutes, stirring. Add the potatoes, squash, and mustard and stir to combine. Add the beer and stir, scraping up any browned bits on the bottom of the pot, until the mixture is smooth. Continue to cook until the beer is reduced by half, then pour in the broth, bring the mixture to a simmer, and cover. Decrease the heat to low and simmer gently, stirring every so often, until the potatoes are tender, 30 to 35 minutes. Add more broth or water if the soup becomes overly thick.

Meanwhile, bring a medium pot of lightly salted water to a boil. Cook the egg noodles according to the package instructions until al dente. Drain, rinse with cold water, and toss with a few drops of oil to prevent sticking. Set aside.

When ready to serve, stir in the sour cream and season the soup with salt and pepper. In a medium skillet over medium-low heat, heat just enough oil to cover the bottom of the pan. Add the meatballs and slowly reheat them, browning on all sides. Work in batches if necessary. When hot, add the meatballs to the soup. When ready to serve, stir in the parsley and cooked egg noodles, and heat for 5 minutes. Ladle into shallow bowls, and serve immediately.

The soup base (minus the meatballs and pasta) can be made in advance and stored in an airtight container in the refrigerator for up to 5 days. (If you don't plan on eating all the soup at once, wait to add the noodles to the entire batch. They end up soaking up too much soup when stored, so add them just before serving.) I don't recommend freezing this soup.

Cauliflower Soup

with Golden Garlic and Toasted Seeds

It's rare to find a vegetable that can transform into something so rich, comforting, and creamy without a drop of cream, but cauliflower does just that, making this soup completely vegan. You can puree it as smooth as you like, though I personally like to leave it a little chunky. A sprinkle of toasted seeds and a scattering of fried sliced garlic on top add just the right amount of crunch.

MAKES 6 SERVINGS

16 large garlic cloves

Extra-virgin olive oil

1 medium head of cauliflower (about 1¾ pounds / 825 g)

Kosher salt and freshly ground black pepper

½ yellow onion, finely chopped

12 ounces (336 g) yellow or Yukon gold potatoes, scrubbed and cut into ½-inch (1 cm) chunks

4 cups (960 g) low-sodium vegetable broth, plus more as needed

4-Seed Sprinkle (page 42), for garnish

In a small saucepan over medium heat, add 10 of the whole garlic cloves and enough olive oil to cover. When the oil begins to bubble, decrease the heat to low and gently cook until the garlic is very tender, about 15 minutes. With a slotted spoon, transfer the garlic to a bowl. Reserve the garlic oil in the pan.

Discard any cauliflower leaves, then chop the cauliflower florets and stem into 1-inch (2.5 cm) pieces. In a large Dutch oven over medium-high heat, warm 2 tablespoons of the reserved garlic oil. Working in two batches to avoid crowding, add the cauliflower. Cook, stirring once or twice, until nicely browned in spots, about 5 minutes. Transfer the cooked cauliflower to a plate and season with salt and pepper. Repeat with the second batch of cauliflower, adding more oil if needed.

Decrease the heat to medium. Add 2 tablespoons more of the reserved garlic oil. Add the onion and cook, stirring, until golden, about 6 minutes. Add the reserved cauliflower, the cooked whole garlic cloves, the potatoes, and broth. Season generously with salt and pepper. Increase the heat to medium-high, bring to a gentle boil, then decrease the heat to medium-low and simmer gently, stirring occasionally, until the potatoes and cauliflower are very tender, 13 minutes.

Meanwhile, thinly slice the remaining 6 garlic cloves. In the reserved saucepan over medium heat, reheat the remaining garlic oil. Add the sliced garlic and cook, stirring, until golden, about 30 seconds. Remove from the heat and, using a slotted spoon, remove the garlic from the oil and set aside. (Save any remaining oil in an airtight jar for other uses.)

Using an immersion blender, countertop blender, or food processor, blend the soup to the consistency you desire, adding more broth if needed. Taste and season with more salt and pepper if needed.

Ladle the soup into individual bowls. Garnish each with fried garlic slices and the 4-seed sprinkle and serve at once.

The soup can be made in advance and stored in an airtight container in the refrigerator for up to 5 days. The soup base can be stored in the freezer for 2 to 3 months.

NEW CLASSICS

Some of the best evenings we've had entertaining at home have started in the kitchen, in that messy moment right before the meal is ready—when our dinner guests huddle in our kitchen, picking at bits of food as the final touches are added. Their appetite is obvious, and it fills the space with lively conversation and anticipation.

A few years ago, my partner and I began making a concerted effort to invite friends for dinner more often. It's all too easy *not* to entertain at home, one busy day bleeding into the next. Hosting requires energy and planning, not to mention cooking, but with friends like ours, it's all worthwhile.

The recipes in this chapter are the dishes I find myself making time and time again for our dinner guests—simple, traditional Scandinavian dishes. I chose them because they never fail to please. Crispy fish cakes, rich stews, home-smoked fish, fall-apart, tender meats—all made from scratch to conjure up as much good flavor as possible.

Sometimes making good food takes time. Not necessarily active work time, but time, nevertheless. Admittedly, none of the recipes in this chapter are 30-minute meals. But for goodness' sake, the meat needs to braise, the vegetables need to be cut, and the fish needs to smoke, all to make them just right.

The recipes in this chapter have something else in common—they are all modern versions of traditional Scandinavian recipes. The original recipes, as lovely as they were, reflected a specific time or an approach to food that has since shifted. Now legumes and whole grains are added to the mix, not only to stretch a meal further but to add texture, nutrition, and heartiness. And in the best stews, chunks of root vegetables like parsnips, rutabagas, beets, and celery root have replaced some or even all the meat, and they get slow roasted or braised just the same. Good-quality meat is still there, there's just less of it, and it's eaten less often.

I tweaked my recipe for Scandinavian Meatballs (page 194) to replace nearly 50 percent of the meat weight with vegetables—it's still irresistible and so satisfying, but now, with more good ingredients. Vegetable and Bean Hash (page 208)—my plant-based take on *biksemad/pyttipanna,* a Scandinavian hash that's traditionally heavy on meat and potatoes—is perfect for the times when guests are expected and the refrigerator is brimming with vegetables.

There's a reason the dishes in this chapter have become Scandinavian keepsakes: They're simply too good to be forgotten. But that doesn't mean they can't evolve and continue to tug on our heartstrings each time we sit down to enjoy them.

Scandinavian Meatballs

with Shaken Red Currants

We have a running joke at Kantine that whenever we're asked to do catering, all we really have to serve is these meatballs to please our clients. This revamped recipe confirmed exactly what I'd suspected: The meatball base could be made with a lot of vegetables and have a fantastic taste and texture. If you have a meat grinder, grinding the meat yourself (chuck and round for the beef, and shoulder or butt for the pork) can be a fun little project, and if you prefer a pure meat mix with just beef or just pork, that works, too.

The recipe suggests making 2-ounce (56 g) meatballs, but feel free to play with the size as you like. I'm a sucker for things small-size, which is why I love to make at least some of the batch into mini meatballs, about the size of a walnut in its shell. My daughter is the opposite. She loves meatballs that are larger than usual—close to the size of a tennis ball—with a spoonful of Danish Remoulade (page 60) on top! Just be aware that if you deviate from the recipe, you'll have to adjust the frying time accordingly, one way or another, to ensure that the meatball is cooked through by the time it's beautifully browned on the outside. **MAKES 38 MEATBALLS**

- 5 ounces (140 g) crusty bread (stale is fine!), cut into bite-size pieces
- 2 pounds (900 g) ground beef
- 1 pound (454 g) ground pork
- 2 tablespoons kosher salt, plus more as needed
- 1½ pounds (680 g) zucchini, shredded on the large holes of a box grater
- 4 large onions (36 ounces / 900 g), finely chopped
- 3 garlic cloves, minced
- 7 eggs
- ¾ cup (79 g) quick oats
- 1 teaspoon ground allspice, plus more as needed
- Freshly ground black pepper
- Neutral oil, for frying
- Hot and creamy mashed potatoes, for serving
- 1 cup (140 g) Shaken Red Currants (recipe follows) or lingonberry jam, for serving
- Pickled Cucumbers (page 47), for serving

Place the bread in a medium bowl, add just enough water to cover, and set aside to soften for 10 minutes. Then remove the bread and gently squeeze out any excess water. Discard the water and set the bread aside.

In the bowl of a stand mixer fitted with the paddle attachment, combine the ground meats and salt. Beat on medium-high speed until tacky, about 2 minutes. Add the zucchini, onions, garlic, eggs, oats, allspice, and pepper and mix until combined. The meat base can be made ahead and kept refrigerated up to 1 day prior to frying.

I always fry off a small sample before frying an entire batch of a mixture to make sure the seasonings are on point. Heat a medium skillet over medium heat, add a few drops of oil, and brown a tablespoon-size patty of the meat mixture on both sides until cooked through. Let cool slightly. Taste and add more salt, pepper, or allspice to the main batch. Fry off another sample, if necessary.

Line a baking tray with parchment paper and scoop the meatball mix into balls, each weighing about 2 ounces (56 g).

CONTINUED

Wipe out the skillet and return it to medium heat. Add enough oil to just barely cover the bottom of the pan. Heat the oil briefly and, working in batches, add the meatballs to the pan, leaving about ½ inch (1 cm) between. I like to keep these meatballs as round as possible (as Swedes do), but you can flatten them, too, if you prefer. Decrease the heat to medium-low and fry until golden brown on the first side, 2 to 3 minutes, then with tongs, turn the meatballs occasionally until browned on all sides. Transfer the meatballs to an oven-safe dish. (It's a good idea to keep them warm in a 190°F / 90°C oven while you finish frying.) Cook the remaining meatballs in the same fashion, adding more oil as necessary. Serve immediately accompanied by creamy mashed potatoes, shaken red currants, and pickled cucumbers.

The cooked meatballs freeze beautifully for up to a month. I often repurpose leftovers by putting them into Sven's Meatball Soup (page 187).

Shaken Red Currants

At my mother-in-law's summerhouse, red currant bushes were in the far corner of the garden, heavy with fruit in the summer. She wasn't much of a cook, but somehow, a bowl of *rysteribs*—just currants and sugar, gently shaken together—always made the food she served feel more vibrant. The sugar tames the currants' sourness, creating a syrupy glaze that makes them delectable alongside Scandinavian Meatballs, spooned over yogurt, or scattered on a cheese plate. Some people leave the stems on for a pretty presentation, but I prefer them stemmed, ready to eat. They're best made no more than an hour before serving—any longer, and they start to lose their plumped firmness. For sweet preparations, adding a touch of vanilla wouldn't be out of place.

MAKES 1 CUP

1 cup (135 g) fresh red currants

¼ cup (50 g) sugar

Carefully rinse and dry the currants. Remove the stems by pulling the stems through the tines of a fork, collecting the berries beneath in a small bowl or jar. Add the sugar. Gently stir or shake (in a lidded jar) to distribute the sugar. Don't shake too hard or the berries will burst. Let stand at room temperature for 30 to 60 minutes before using.

effortless ways to consume less meat

There are plenty of reasons to eat less meat, whether it's for environmental impact, personal health, animal welfare, or rising food costs. But for those who truly enjoy a meaty meal, cutting it out completely can feel daunting.

It's not just about saying goodbye to the taste of meat. Shifting away from meat can be challenging for many reasons, like cooking for family members with different preferences, making sure you're getting enough protein, or simply not knowing where to start when it comes to cooking with emphasis on a different set of ingredients.

If you're at a place where you're considering reducing your meat consumption, might give you the incentive to make a change.

Buy less meat. As obvious as it may seem, the simplest way to eat less meat is to bring less of it into your home. Be intentional when shopping and let vegetables, grains, and legumes fill your bags instead.

Plan meals ahead of time. Knowing what you plan on cooking can make your intentions easier to achieve and helps avoid defaulting to meat-heavy meals out of habit.

Add in a meat-free Monday. Committing to just one plant-based day per week can be a good starting place. Once you've settled into that, you might feel ready to add more meatless days.

Replace some of the ground meat in recipes with vegetables or legumes. I've done it with many of my recipes, as in the Scandinavian Meatballs with Shaken Red Currants (page 194).

Change the focus. Try turning the meat-centric meal upside down and instead use smaller amounts of meat as a flavor enhancer for your abundance of cooked vegetables.

Consume high-quality meat on rare occasions. When you do eat meat, make it count. Choosing well-raised, flavorful meat for special meals can make you more appreciative of it still being a part of your diet, despite the limitations.

Partner with someone. Making changes together—whether it's with a friend, roommate, or spouse—can help keep you motivated and make cooking more enjoyable.

Get inspired. Borrow vegetable-forward cookbooks from the library, browse recipes online, or explore new ingredients at the market. Expanding your cooking repertoire makes cutting back on meat feel exciting, not restrictive.

Stay informed. Learning about the benefits of reducing meat consumption—whether for health, sustainability, or cost—can make it easier to stick with your choices.

Remember, change doesn't have to happen overnight, and your diet doesn't need to fit neatly into a label like *vegetarian, vegan,* or *pescatarian.* What's important is that it suits *you* and makes sense in *your* life, whatever your reasons may be.

Trout and Cod Fish Cakes

with Celery and Radish Relish

This recipe came to life in my home kitchen before becoming a staple at Kantine. The combination of flesh from a large flaked white fish and an oily fish such as trout or salmon is simply gorgeous. Have a look at the Monterey Bay Aquarium's seafood guide to buy fish that's sustainable and safe to eat. Feel free to swap out the celery and radish relish with Remoulade (page 60) if you prefer a more classic condiment. MAKES 12 LARGE CAKES

FISH CAKES

- 1 pound (454 g) boneless, skinless fresh trout or salmon
- 14 ounces (392 g) boneless, skinless fresh Pacific cod or rockfish
- 2 teaspoons kosher salt, plus more as needed
- 1 tablespoon Dijon mustard
- 2 teaspoons grainy mustard
- ½ cup (125 g) sour cream
- ¼ cup (50 g) mayonnaise
- 1 tablespoon chopped fresh dill
- 1 tablespoon chopped fresh chives
- 1 egg
- 1 tablespoon all-purpose flour
- Neutral oil, for frying
- Freshly ground black pepper

RELISH

- 4 celery stalks (8 ounces / 224 g), finely diced and leaves sliced
- 1 bunch of red radishes (about 8 radishes), trimmed and finely diced
- ¼ cup (25 g) toasted sliced almonds (see Toasting Nuts and Seeds, page 42; optional)
- 2 tablespoons extra-virgin olive oil
- 1 tablespoon fresh lemon juice
- Kosher salt and freshly ground black pepper

Prepare the fish cakes. Cut about 2 ounces of each type of fish into ½-inch (1 cm) cubes and reserve. Put the remainder of the fish into the bowl of a food processor with 2 teaspoons of the salt. Pulse until no chunks are visible and the mixture is stiff and sticky, scraping the bowl down with a rubber spatula, if necessary. Transfer to a large bowl and stir in the mustards, sour cream, mayonnaise, dill, chives, egg, and flour, along with the reserved cubed fish. Cover with plastic wrap and refrigerate for 30 minutes or up to 1 day.

Meanwhile, make the relish. In a medium bowl, stir together the celery, radishes, almonds, olive oil, and lemon juice and season with salt and pepper. Refrigerate until ready to serve, up to 2 days.

I always fry off a small sample before frying an entire batch of a mixture to make sure the seasonings are on point. Heat a medium skillet over medium heat, add a few drops of oil, and brown a tablespoon-size patty of the fish cake mix on both sides, until cooked through, 1 to 2 minutes per side. Let cool slightly. Taste and add more salt or pepper to the main batch, if needed. Fry off another sample, if necessary.

Line a baking tray with parchment paper. Portion the fish cake base into 12 round patties about 3 ounces (84 g) each—I like to use a scale for precision.

Wipe out the skillet and return it to medium heat. Add enough oil to just barely cover the bottom of the pan. Heat the oil briefly and, working in batches, add as many cakes to the pan as will fit without touching. Fry until golden brown, 2 to 3 minutes per side.

The beauty of these cakes is their delicate texture, so be gentle and avoid moving them more than necessary. Once browned on both sides, transfer the cakes to an oven-safe dish. (It's a good idea to keep them warm in a 190°F / 90°C oven while you finish frying.) Cook the remaining cakes in the same fashion, adding more oil as necessary. Serve immediately, accompanied by the celery and radish relish.

Fried fish cakes can be stored in an airtight container in the refrigerator for up to 3 days, and they are also quite tasty cold!

Oven-Smoked Salmon
with Horseradish-Dill Cream

City living rarely comes with space for an outdoor smoker, but with this oven method of smoking, there's no need for one. While the smoke smell will likely linger in your kitchen for a day or two (some of us actually enjoy that!), the process itself couldn't be easier.

I prefer to brine the fish the day before smoking, so it has ample time to dry before being smoked. Getting the chips really going before adding them to the oven is especially important at the start, since that's when the salmon absorbs the most smoky flavor. The result is tender, flavorful fish with just the right amount of smokiness—no backyard needed. **MAKES 8 SERVINGS**

BRINED SALMON

2 cups (475 g) boiling water

1 cup (150 g) kosher salt

¾ cup (160 g) sugar

1 cup (185 g) ice cubes

2 cups (475 g) cold water

2 bay leaves

1 teaspoon black peppercorns

1 skin-on wild salmon fillet (about 2 pounds / 900 g), pin bones removed

2 to 3 handfuls dry hardwood smoking chips (such as apple- or cherrywood)

HORSERADISH-DILL CREAM

1 cup (260 g) crème fraîche or sour cream

2 tablespoons peeled and finely grated fresh horseradish

2 teaspoons fresh lemon juice

3 sprigs of dill, stemmed and leaves chopped

Kosher salt

Rye or other seeded flatbread crackers, for serving

Brine the fish. In a 9 by 13-inch (23 by 33 cm) baking dish, stir together the boiling water with the salt and sugar until they dissolve. Add the ice and stir until the ice melts and the mixture cools. Add the cold water, bay leaves, and peppercorns and stir to combine. Place the salmon skin side up in the brine. Top with a few small plates to fully submerge the salmon in the brine. Cover and refrigerate for 4 to 8 hours.

Place a wire rack on top of a large baking tray. Remove the salmon from the brine, rinse with cold water, and blot dry with paper towels. Place the fish skin side down on the rack and refrigerate, uncovered, until it looks dry and shiny, at least 4 hours but preferably 24 hours.

When ready to smoke, take the fish out of the refrigerator to come to room temperature while you prepare the oven.

Position one rack in the lower third of the oven and another in the upper third of the oven. On the upper rack, place an inverted baking tray (it will help tent the smoke over the salmon below). Preheat the oven to 200°F (95°C). Line a large cast-iron pan with aluminum foil. (Turn on your exhaust fan and open the windows.) Place the foil-lined pan on the stovetop and add a big handful of the dry wood chips. Heat over medium-high heat until the wood chips are smoldering and smoking.

Place the baking tray holding the wire rack and fish on the lower oven rack. Place the foil-lined pan with the smoking wood chips underneath, directly on the oven floor. Shut the door and smoke until the fish is cooked through and smoked to your liking, about 2 hours. (Check on the chips every 30 minutes and, if they burn out and/or are no longer smoking, repeat the process on the stovetop, adding more if necessary.)

Make the horseradish cream. In a small bowl, stir together the crème fraîche, horseradish, lemon juice, and dill. Season with salt. Cover and refrigerate until ready to use.

The smoked fish can be served warm, straight from the oven, or room temperature, accompanied by the crackers and horseradish cream. To store, wrap tightly and refrigerate for up to 5 days.

Autumn Duck Stew

with Chanterelles and Farro

In Scandinavia, duck is usually reserved for the December holidays, typically served as a whole roast. It also makes an appearance in November on Mortens Aften, or Saint Martin's Eve, a Danish tradition where roast duck or goose is eaten in honor of Saint Martin, who supposedly hid in a goose pen to avoid being ordained as a bishop—go figure!

This recipe is different in that only duck legs are used and braised until they are fall-apart tender. The grain is variable—wheat berries or barley would be great substitutes. **MAKES 4 TO 6 SERVINGS**

- ⅔ cup (20 g) dried porcini or mixed mushrooms
- 1 cup (240 g) boiling water
- 3 tablespoons unsalted butter
- 2 tablespoons extra-virgin olive oil
- 1 small yellow onion (4 ounces / 112 g), finely chopped
- 2 medium carrots (5 ounces / 140 g), scrubbed and diced
- 3 medium parsnips (7½ ounces / 210 g), scrubbed and diced
- Kosher salt and freshly ground black pepper
- 2 garlic cloves, minced
- 1 large sprig of thyme
- 2 bay leaves
- ½ cup (120 g) dry red wine
- 4 to 5 cups (960 to 1200 g) good-quality low-sodium chicken broth, plus more as needed
- 3 bone-in, skin-on duck legs (about 1½ pounds / 725 g), preferably Liberty duck
- ¾ cup (4 ounces / 115 g) pearled farro
- 8 ounces (225 g) fresh chanterelle, oyster, or cremini mushrooms, brushed clean and cut into bite-size pieces
- Chopped fresh tarragon, for garnish

In a heatproof bowl, combine the dried mushrooms and boiling water and let stand for 30 minutes. Drain the mushrooms through a fine-mesh sieve set over a bowl. Set the liquid aside. Finely chop the rehydrated mushrooms and set aside separately.

In a large Dutch oven over medium-high heat, melt 2 tablespoons of the butter with the oil. Add the onion, carrot, and parsnips, season with salt and pepper, and cook, stirring occasionally, until lightly golden, about 5 minutes. Add the rehydrated mushrooms, garlic, thyme, and bay leaves and stir to combine. Stir in the wine and simmer just until thickened, about 1 minute. Add 4 cups (960 g) of the broth, the reserved mushroom liquid, and 1 teaspoon salt, then nestle the duck legs in the liquid. Bring to a boil, then decrease the heat to low to maintain a gentle simmer, cover partially, and cook, stirring occasionally, until the duck is very tender, about 2 hours.

Transfer the duck legs to a cutting board. Add the farro to the stew, increase the heat to medium, and bring to a boil. Decrease the heat to medium-low, cover, and simmer until the farro is tender, about 15 minutes.

Meanwhile, pull the duck meat from the bones and tear it into bite-size pieces; discard the skin and bones. Using a large metal spoon, skim off any fat from the surface of the soup. Return the shredded duck meat to the stew and keep warm over low heat. The stew will be fairly thick and will thicken further as it cools; thin with additional broth to achieve the consistency you desire. Taste and season with salt and pepper.

When ready to serve, in a medium skillet over medium-high heat, melt the remaining 1 tablespoon butter. Add the chanterelles and a pinch of salt and cook, stirring, until browned and tender, about 5 minutes.

Ladle the stew into individual bowls, top each bowl with the chanterelles, dividing them evenly, then garnish with a sprinkle of tarragon. Serve.

The stew base can be stored in an airtight container in the refrigerator for 3 days and in the freezer for 1 month.

Beer-Braised Lamb

with Winter Vegetables and Kale Cream

On rainy days in San Francisco, this lamb stew always hits the spot. Braising the meat until tender takes time, but the aromas that fill the house in the meantime make the wait a joyful one.

MAKES 6 SERVINGS

STEW

2 pounds (900 g) boneless lamb shoulder or top round, fat chunks and sinew removed, cut into 2-inch (5 cm) chunks

Kosher salt and freshly ground black pepper

⅓ cup (42 g) all-purpose flour

¼ cup (55 g) plus 2 tablespoons neutral oil

2 medium onions, cut into ½-inch (1 cm) dice (12 ounces / 336 g)

4 to 5 medium carrots, scrubbed and cut into 1-inch (2.5 cm) chunks (12 ounces / 336 g)

3 to 4 medium parsnips, scrubbed and cut into 1-inch (2.5 cm) chunks (9 ounces / 252 g)

4 medium russet potatoes, scrubbed and cut into 2-inch (5 cm) chunks (32 ounces / 896 g)

2 cups (480 g) lager (such as Heineken or Grolsch)

1½ cups (360 g) vegetable broth

2 dried bay leaves

4 sprigs of thyme

1 pound (454 g) savoy cabbage, stemmed and cut into 3-inch (7.5 cm) chunks

5 sprigs of dill, for serving

KALE CREAM

1 large bunch of lacinato or curly green kale (9 ounces / 252 g), stemmed and coarsely chopped

1 tablespoon Dijon mustard

3 tablespoons mayonnaise

½ cup (125 g) sour cream

Kosher salt and freshly ground black pepper

Make the stew. Place the meat into a large bowl, season with salt and pepper, then add the flour and toss to coat thoroughly. Heat a large heavy-bottomed skillet (ideally one with 2-inch / 5 cm or higher sides and a lid) over medium-high heat. Add ¼ cup (55 g) of the oil. Shake the excess flour off the meat, place into the hot oil, and brown on all sides, about 6 minutes. Decrease the heat if the bottom of the skillet is beginning to darken. Transfer the meat to a large bowl and set aside.

Add the remaining 2 tablespoons oil to the skillet along with the onions, carrots, and parsnips. Cook until the vegetables have softened slightly and gotten some color, about 4 minutes. Return the browned lamb to the skillet along with the potatoes. Pour the beer in and bring to a simmer. As the beer heats, use a wooden spoon to scrape up any browned bits on the bottom of the pot—they have so much flavor! Cook over medium heat until the beer is reduced by half, then add the broth and just enough water to cover the lamb and vegetables. Bring to a boil again, throw in the bay leaves and thyme, make sure everything is submerged in liquid, and put a lid on it. Let the stew simmer until the meat is still just slightly tough, about 45 minutes.

Meanwhile, make the kale cream. In a food processor, combine the kale, mustard, mayonnaise, and sour cream. Pulse to make a slightly chunky, green-hued sauce. Season with salt and pepper and refrigerate until ready to serve. (The kale cream can be made 1 day in advance and stored in the refrigerator.)

Finish the stew. Add the cabbage, put the lid back on, and simmer until the lamb is very tender, an additional 20 to 30 minutes. Remove the bay leaves and thyme sprigs and season with salt and pepper.

To serve, divide the stew among six shallow bowls, topping with a bit of dill, and serve immediately accompanied by a bowl of kale cream.

Vegetable and Bean Hash

This kind of dish knows no borders—nearly every cuisine has a way of turning leftover vegetables into something hearty and satisfying. In Scandinavia, versions like *pyttipanna* in Sweden, *pytt i panne* in Norway, and *biksemad* in Denmark are typically made with leftover roast meat, potatoes, onions, and whatever else is on hand. This meatless version relies on root vegetables and beans. I'm having a hard time thinking of a vegetable that isn't suitable for this dish, but nothing comes to mind! My favorites include carrots, parsnips, zucchini, celery root, sweet potato, and brussels sprouts. Together with the pickled condiments and garnishes, it hits all the flavor sensations: umami, sweet, salty, bitter, and sour.

I've called for kidney beans or chickpeas, but really, any of your favorite beans will work here, and if you'd rather add meat, chunks of leftover duck confit or roast pork are both excellent options. If your vegetables and potatoes aren't already cooked, roast or air-fry them until soft before proceeding. Serve with pickled cucumbers, pickled beets, or even ketchup for that perfect balance of flavors. **MAKES 4 SERVINGS**

¼ cup (55 g) neutral oil, plus more for frying eggs

⅔ cup (90 g) chopped yellow onion

12 ounces (336 g) cremini mushrooms, thickly sliced

Kosher salt and freshly ground black pepper

1 pound (454 g) cooked vegetables (see headnote), cut into bite-size pieces

9 ounces (252 g) boiled or roasted potato, cut into bite-size pieces

9 ounces (252 g) cooked kidney beans or chickpeas

4 eggs

1 bunch of chives, chopped

Pickled Cucumbers (page 47), for serving

Pickled Beets (page 48), for serving

Ketchup, for serving

Heat a large Dutch oven over medium heat. Add 1 tablespoon of the oil and the onion. Cook, stirring occasionally, until lightly golden, about 3 minutes. Add the mushrooms, season with salt and pepper, and cook, stirring often, until they begin to soften and release their liquid, 3 to 4 minutes. Pour the onion-mushroom mixture into a bowl. Set aside.

Return the pot to the stovetop and add 2 tablespoons of the oil, followed by the vegetables and potato. Season with salt and pepper and cook, stirring occasionally, until everything is heated through and slightly browned, 4 to 5 minutes. Add the beans as well as the reserved onion-mushroom mixture. Cook until heated through, 2 to 3 minutes. Keep warm over low heat while you prepare the eggs.

Just before serving, heat a large skillet over medium heat. Add the remaining tablespoon of oil to the pan, then break the eggs into the pan, staying close to the pan so your yolks don't break. Season with salt and pepper and cook until the egg whites are opaque but the yolks are still runny, 2 minutes.

Arrange the hash on four plates, topping each with a fried egg and chives. Serve immediately with pickled cucumbers, pickled beets, and/or ketchup alongside.

STAUB
STAUB

Beef Kalops Stew
with Pickled Beets

This Swedish beef stew is built on the warming depth of allspice, a spice that lives up to its name, as it tastes like a mix of cloves, cinnamon, and nutmeg. It gives *kalops* its signature flavor and enhances the comforting richness of the slow-cooked beef and carrots.

This stew is traditionally served with boiled potatoes and pickled beets. It's the kind of meal that is good to make in a large batch (an Instant Pot would probably be great for this), often tastes better the day after, and can be frozen for a later date. Choose a grass-fed, well-marbled beef chuck, which will break down into the most tender chunks as it simmers. **MAKES 4 TO 6 SERVINGS**

- 10 whole allspice berries
- 2½ pounds (1.1 kg) beef chuck roast, cut into 1½-inch (4 cm) cubes
- Kosher salt and freshly ground black pepper
- 2 tablespoons neutral oil, plus more as needed
- 2 tablespoons unsalted butter
- 1 medium yellow onion (6 ounces / 168 g), diced
- ⅓ cup (42 g) all-purpose flour
- 3 cups (720 g) good-quality beef or chicken broth, plus more as needed
- 4 medium carrots (10 ounces / 288 g), scrubbed and cut into 1-inch (2.5 cm) pieces (halved lengthwise if thick)
- 4 bay leaves
- 1 tablespoon red wine vinegar
- Fresh flat-leaf parsley, torn, for garnish
- Boiled small yellow potatoes, warm, for serving
- Pickled Beets (page 48), for serving

Place the allspice berries in a coffee filter and tie shut with a piece of twine. Season the beef generously all over with salt and pepper. Heat a large Dutch oven over medium-high heat and add the oil. Working in batches to avoid overcrowding, sear the beef cubes, turning once, until nicely browned on two sides, about 8 minutes. Transfer the meat to a plate and set aside. Repeat with the remaining beef, adding more oil if needed.

Decrease the heat to medium and add the butter to the pot. When melted, add the onion. Cook, stirring and scraping up any browned bits on the bottom of the pot, until tender and golden, about 5 minutes. Add the flour and stir until well combined, then cook for another 2 minutes, stirring. Add the broth and stir, scraping the bottom of the pot again, until the mixture is smooth. Add the carrots, bay leaves, allspice in filter, and the reserved beef and juices and stir to combine. Cover and bring to a simmer, then decrease the heat to low and simmer gently, stirring every so often, until the meat is very tender, 2 to 2½ hours. Add more broth or water if the stew becomes overly thick, or remove the lid and simmer uncovered if the stew is too thin for your liking. When the meat is tender and the soup has reached your desired consistency, stir in the vinegar.

To serve, remove the bay leaves and allspice. Ladle into wide shallow bowls and garnish with parsley. Serve the boiled potatoes and pickled beets alongside.

The stew can be stored in an airtight container in the refrigerator for up to 4 days or in the freezer for up to 2 months.

Lamb with Anchovies, Spruce, and Parsley Root

This recipe is based on a classic Swedish combination: lamb and anchovies. The resulting dish is rich and intensely meaty, with extra depth and umami from the anchovies melting into the meat. It's fabulous for serving at larger gatherings, where I like to arrange a large platter with the tender meat, top it with the parsley root, and then surround it with a few big bowls with a colorful grain salad, a hearty green salad, a cold sauce (see A Cold Sauce Matrix, page 62, for inspiration), and some crusty bread for mopping up the broth.

When shopping for lamb, look for fresh, domestically raised lamb, which tends to be milder and more tender than imported frozen lamb. If you prefer a pink roast instead of a slow-cooked braise, you can shorten the cooking time, though you won't get the same fall-apart tenderness.

If you're preparing this recipe in the spring, and you live near a wooded area, this might be the perfect opportunity to forage tender, citrusy spruce tips to flavor your roast. And if parsley root is new to you, you're in for a treat. It resembles a pale, slender parsnip (or white carrot), but has a milder, earthier flavor with a hint of parsley (no surprise, I suppose), celery and carrot. If parsley root is hard to find, use parsnip instead. Freeze any leftover broth for future lamb preparations—it's too good to waste. **MAKES 10 TO 12 SERVINGS**

- 10 pounds (4.5 kg) fresh lamb shoulder or boneless leg of lamb
- 8 to 10 anchovy fillets in olive oil, drained (reserve some of the oil) and cut in half
- 3 garlic cloves, peeled and cut into small matchsticks
- 30 spruce tips (see A Forager at Heart, page 239), or 4 large sprigs of rosemary, cut into ¾-inch (2 cm) pieces
- 2 tablespoons olive oil
- Kosher salt and freshly ground black pepper
- 1 quart (960 g) unsalted chicken bone broth
- 2 cups (480 g) white wine
- 9 medium parsley roots (about 1 pound 9 ounces / 700 g), scrubbed and cut into 1-inch (2.5 cm) slices
- Lemon wedges, for serving

Preheat the oven to 450°F (230°C).

Trim any areas of excessive fat or sinew off the lamb shoulder (a thin layer of fat is completely fine). Using a small knife, make 15 to 20 slits all over in the meat, large enough to insert the first inch (2.5 cm) of your pinky finger. In each slit, insert an anchovy half, followed by a piece or two of garlic, and a spruce tip. When all the holes have been filled, rub the olive oil all over the outside of the meat. Season the meat on all sides with 2 teaspoons of salt and several grinds of pepper.

Place any remaining spruce tips on the bottom of a roasting pan and place the meat fat side up on top. Roast for 30 minutes. This will help create a nice crust and add flavor. Decrease the oven temperature to 350°F (175°C). Add the broth and wine to the pan, cover with foil or a lid, and place it back in the oven to slow roast for 4½ hours.

Remove the cover and toss the parsley root into the bottom of the pan, replace the cover, return the pan to the oven and roast for 30 more minutes. At this point, the parsley root should be tender and the meat should be fork-tender. If not, continue to roast for another 30 minutes. When the parsley root is tender, fish it out with a slotted spoon and set aside. Remove the covering and immediately switch the oven to broil. Broil the roast until lightly browned, 5 to 10 minutes more. Keep a keen eye on it!

Let the lamb rest for 10 to 15 minutes before carefully transferring it to a serving platter, surrounded by the parsley root. The meat is extremely tender and tastes amazing with a squeeze of fresh lemon juice.

Roast Pork Belly
with Chard and Ramps

Denmark's national dish, *stegt flæsk,* is a favorite home-cooked meal. The dish's name literally means "fried pork," a true testament to the Danish language's history of being straightforward. It's pan-fried, thick-cut pork belly that is traditionally served with boiled potatoes and a thick, milk-based, parsley-flecked sauce. The meat, when prepared well, is very crispy (though not hard) and tender. Did I mention it being ridiculously delicious? There are restaurants in Denmark that offer all-you-can-eat-belly—something I would never try, afraid of what too much of a good thing might be like.

The traditional way to cook the meat is on the stovetop—a process that not only requires your undivided attention for a good while but also ends up covering every kitchen surface in grease and leaving the house smelling like fat for days. I have often wanted to serve it for guests but shied away for the aforementioned reasons.

In my version, the pork belly is rubbed with spices before being slow roasted. Once the roasted belly has gotten cold in the refrigerator—likely the following day—it can be sliced and pan-fried to perfection, which takes only a fraction of the time of the old method. There's a lot less hot fat flying around, most of the preparation time is hands-off, and the meat is more flavorful, thanks to the spices.

When buying pork belly, look for one on the thicker side, with a good balance of fat and meat. The minerally chard cuts through the fattiness, making each bite balanced.

In the backyard of my mother's house in Ohio, there's a large patch of ramps that I just happened to discover the last time I visited her there. Now, whenever they are in season, I can't help but wish she were still here. The ramp season is very short, so try to catch them while you can! **MAKES 4 TO 6 SERVINGS**

- 2 teaspoons fennel seeds
- 2 teaspoons black peppercorns
- 4 bay leaves
- 4½ to 5 pounds (2 to 2.25 kg) skinless fresh pork belly
- Kosher salt and freshly ground black pepper
- 1 tablespoon olive oil
- 24 fresh ramps, white and green parts cut into 2-inch (5 cm) segments (or 2 bunches of scallions)
- 1 large bunch of chard (about 7 ounces / 196 g), stemmed, stems chopped, leaves left in large pieces
- Hot and creamy mashed potatoes, for serving

Preheat the oven to 450°F (230°C).

In a mortar or spice grinder, coarsely grind the fennel, peppercorns, and bay leaves.

Inspect the meat, removing and discarding any visible large chunks of fat or sinew. Season both sides of the meat generously with 2 teaspoons of salt. With a knife, cut a ⅛-inch (3 mm) deep crisscross pattern into the fat on the top of the belly. Flip the belly over and rub the ground spices into the meat. Place the belly fat side up in a roasting pan and transfer to the oven. Bake uncovered for 30 minutes, then decrease the oven temperature to 350°F (175°C). Slow roast for 2½ hours, then turn the temperature back up to 450°F (230°C) and roast for 15 minutes more. This higher temperature crisps the meat up, creating a slight crust on the top. Remove the belly from the oven. (Even though it is fully cooked at this point, it's what happens moving forward that makes this dish outstanding!) Let the meat cool to room

CONTINUED

temperature. Wrap and refrigerate the meat until cold, a minimum of 3 hours or up to 3 days in advance.

When ready to serve, cut the belly (parallel to the grains of the meat) into thirds. Then, starting from the short side of the rectangle, cut the belly (perpendicular to the grain) into ½-inch (1 cm) thick slices.

Preheat the oven to 190°F (90°C). Line an oven-safe dish with paper towels.

In a large skillet over medium heat, cover the bottom of the pan with a layer of sliced meat (no oil needed). Fry the pieces until crispy and browned, pouring off some of the melted fat if a lot accumulates, until it resembles a crispy, golden, thick piece of bacon. (It's a good idea to keep the finished meat warm in a 190°F / 90°C oven while you finish frying.) Cook the remaining slices in the same fashion.

Last, prepare the ramps and chard. In a medium skillet over medium heat, warm the olive oil. Add the ramps and give them a few minutes alone in the pan, so that they are flecked with dark scorched spots. Add the chard stems and cook, stirring occasionally, until they have softened, 3 to 4 minutes. Add the chard leaves and a few drops of water and stir continuously until the leaves just begin to wilt. Season lightly with salt and immediately transfer to a serving dish and serve together with the fried pork and creamy mashed potatoes.

smörgåsbord: from side table to dinner table

Ask an American what *smörgåsbord* is, and they most likely will describe something very different from what a Swede might answer. Smörgåsbord is not a jumbled all-you-can-pile-on-your-plate buffet. In Sweden, it is a carefully curated meal, with an order to each course and an unspoken etiquette dictated by tradition.

Smörgåsbord wasn't always so refined. It started on the sidelines, and in this case, literally on a side table. In medieval Sweden, aristocrats would set up a *brännvinsbord* (schnapps table), a small, separate side table stocked with bread, butter, cheese, pickled herring, cold cuts, and, as the name suggests, *brännvin* (Scandinavian schnapps) before dinner. It was a casual, predinner custom with a similar gathering effect as an aperitif, though in some cases, men and women would convene in separate rooms, playing cards and socializing for hours before the actual meal began.

By the seventeenth century, the schnapps table migrated from the side table to the dinner table, expanding in both variety and importance. It was no longer just an opening snack but a full spread where guests could help themselves to a variety of cold dishes before moving on to warm courses. By the time Sweden introduced smörgåsbord to the world at the 1939 New York World's Fair, the term had taken on a life of its own. From that point forward, *smörgåsbord* became shorthand—especially in the United States—for any large buffet-style meal, even when the food isn't Swedish at all.

Harvest Braise

with Root Vegetables, Mushrooms, and Barley

This braise was inspired by *lapskaus,* the Norwegian meat and vegetable stew that is so warming and satisfying, especially when it's cold outside. I wanted to create a vegetarian version that felt just as hearty so I chose ingredients that can handle a long, slow cook, letting the flavors meld into something special. When it came time to test the recipe, my dear friend Jennifer happily took on the task. She's vegan, so she left off the crème fraîche, but the horseradish still worked wonders to liven up each bowl. I like this best with Seedy Crispbread (page 225) with a good smear of butter for a truly comforting meal. **MAKES 4 TO 6 SERVINGS**

- 1 teaspoon juniper berries
- 1 teaspoon black peppercorns
- 3 tablespoons olive oil
- 4 or 5 medium shallots (about 5 ounces / 150 g), cut into ½-inch (1 cm) chunks
- 3 garlic cloves, minced
- 3 tablespoons all-purpose flour
- 1 cup (240 g) dry white wine
- 4 cups (960 g) low-sodium vegetable or chicken broth, plus more as needed
- 2 to 3 medium parsnips (about 8 ounces / 224 g), scrubbed and cut into 1-inch (2.5 cm) chunks
- 2 to 3 medium carrots (about 8 ounces / 224 g), scrubbed and cut into 1-inch (2.5 cm) chunks
- 12 ounces (336 g) small creamer potatoes, scrubbed and cut into 1-inch (2.5 cm) chunks
- 1 medium celery root (about 12 ounces / 336 g), peeled and cut into 1-inch (2.5 cm) chunks
- 12 ounces (336 g) cremini mushrooms, thickly sliced
- 2 sprigs of thyme
- Kosher salt and freshly ground black pepper
- ¾ cup (150 g) pearled barley
- Crème fraîche, for serving
- Freshly grated horseradish or horseradish in vinegar, for serving
- Seedy Crispbread (page 225), for serving

In a mortar or spice grinder, grind the juniper berries and peppercorns to a medium-fine grind. Set aside.

Heat a large Dutch oven over medium heat. Add the olive oil and shallots. Cook, stirring occasionally, until lightly golden, about 4 minutes. Add the garlic and cook just until fragrant. Add the ground spices and the flour and cook, stirring, until well combined. Stir in the wine, scraping up any browned bits on the bottom of the pot, until smooth and the mixture thickens, about 1 minute. Add the broth, parsnips, carrots, potatoes, celery root, mushrooms, thyme, and 2 teaspoons salt. Stir to combine.

Increase the heat to high, partially cover, and bring to a boil, then decrease the heat to low and simmer, stirring frequently to keep it from burning on the bottom, until the vegetables are tender but not falling apart, about 30 minutes. Add the barley and cook, covered, until the vegetables and barley are very tender, about 20 minutes more. Add more broth or water if the stew becomes overly thick or remove the lid and let simmer uncovered if it is too thin for your liking. Taste and season with more salt and pepper as needed.

To serve, remove the thyme sprigs. Ladle into bowls and serve with crème fraîche and/or horseradish, and I highly recommend accompanying it with seedy crispbread.

THOR HEYERDAHL · AKU-AKU
4 BINDS LEKSIKON

SIMPLE BREADS AND SWEET TREATS

Not long after my family and I moved to San Francisco, my son's school began organizing a fundraiser and looking for items to auction off. Another parent who was also married to a Dane suggested we host a Danish open-faced sandwich (smørrebrød) dinner at her house. It sounded like fun. (And, yes, I know smørrebrød is typically a lunch thing, but we decided the school could survive a little rule-bending.) The event sold out fast—perhaps because we'd promised aquavit? My friend and I agreed to serve two courses of smørrebrød followed by Flødeboller (page 244), or Danish meringue puffs. We felt confident that with so much good food (and drink!) this was going to be a blast!

When the day of the event arrived, there were tons of things to take care of, and just as the first guests rang the doorbell, I was dipping the last puff into melted dark chocolate. What a relief!

I picked up the tray and briskly walked out of the kitchen to stash them somewhere safe. As I turned the corner, I fell over a low bench that was blocked from my view by the tray. The cream puffs went flying, only to hit the wall. They were beyond salvaging. I stood in the hallway for a moment, bewildered.

Normally, when catastrophe strikes, I curse in Danish. But this time, another word came to mind, and it helped me turn the corner—mentally, this time—and move forward: *pyt*.

In Danish, *pyt* (pronounced püt") is one of those words (like *hygge*) that doesn't translate directly, but it's a way of saying, "Oh well. Let it go." Danish children learn it in preschool when they fall and skin their knees, or when one of the eyes on their favorite stuffed animal falls off. Adults use it as well, as a mantra to not sweat the small stuff, especially things out of one's control.

Another friend who was attending dashed to the store for heavy cream and frozen raspberries, and with the chocolate left over from the puffs, I made Raspberry "Silk" with Dark Chocolate (page 256)—a simple dessert that comes together in a flash. With everyone's bellies full of smørrebrød, aquavit, and now dessert, there wasn't a dry eye in the room. (Okay, maybe I was the only one tearing up, grateful that the evening was a success.)

So now you've heard about two of the sweet recipes in this chapter, but savory bakes have their place here, too. Whether you're looking for an easy-to-make, sliceable loaf like Malted Sandwich Bread (page 233), a flourless Seedy Crispbread (page 225) or Golden Potato Buns (page 226) to make a round of Scandinavian-Inspired Hot Dogs (see page 230), this chapter will serve you well.

Seedy Crispbread

An alternative to classic Swedish crispbread, this flourless version is addictively good. The "glue" of egg whites, water, and flaxseeds binds everything together, creating a perfectly crisp texture. It's great with creamy cheese (I love it with Cowgirl Creamery's Mt Tam), avocado and tomato, or soft scrambled eggs. Stored in an airtight container, it will last for weeks—but I honestly wouldn't know since it never sticks around that long. **MAKES ONE 12 BY 16-INCH (30 BY 40 CM) CRISPBREAD**

- ¾ cup (115 g) flaxseeds
- 3 egg whites
- ⅓ cup (80 g) water
- 1 cup (148 g) sunflower seeds
- ¼ cup (40 g) pumpkin seeds
- ¼ cup (40 g) sesame seeds
- ½ teaspoon kosher salt, plus more for finishing

The night before you plan to bake the crispbread, stir together the flaxseed, egg whites, and water in a small, covered container and refrigerate until the next day.

Preheat the oven to 300°F (150°C). Cut two pieces of parchment paper into 12 by 16-inch (30 by 40 cm) rectangles.

In a food processor, pulse to coarsely chop the sunflower seeds, pumpkin seeds, and sesame seeds; about twelve quick pulses should be sufficient. Pour the chopped seeds into a medium bowl and add the flaxseed–egg white mixture and salt. Stir to combine.

On your countertop, dump the mixture into the center of one of the pieces of parchment. Using an offset spatula, spread the seed mixture into an even layer, completely covering the parchment. Place the second sheet of parchment on top and very gently roll with a rolling pin to an even thickness.

Slide the bread (parchment and all) onto a 13 by 18-inch (33 by 46 cm) baking tray. Carefully remove the top piece of parchment and scrape off any seeds that have stuck to the paper—use them to patch any holes or thin spots in the bread, again with the help of an offset spatula. Sprinkle a pinch of salt over the seed mixture.

Bake until crunchy and curled on the edges, about 60 minutes. Using the parchment, gently flip the crispbread over on the baking tray so the "top" of the bread is touching the tray directly and the "bottom" is now face up and covered by parchment. Turn off the oven and return the tray to the oven to dry the bread out even more, and leave until both the oven and bread are completely cooled, 1½ to 2 hours.

To serve, peel away the parchment, then break the crispbread into large pieces.

The crispbread can be stored in an airtight container for up to 3 weeks. (If it softens a little, recrisp it in a 300°F / 150°C oven for about 20 minutes.)

Golden Potato Buns

These are hands down my favorite hot dog buns. There's something about adding potatoes to the dough that really improves their texture. Shoot, I'll even eat these buns without the hot dog! The golden color comes from using yellow-fleshed creamer potatoes, but if you have another type of leftover potato you want to use up, that'll work just fine. The potato skins are intentionally left on since I like the flecks of skin in the dough. These buns take time, but the active work is minimal, making them perfect for a day spent at home. See Scandinavian-Inspired Hot Dogs (page 230) for ways to fill your buns. **MAKES 8 BUNS**

5 ounces (140 g) creamer potatoes, skins on, scrubbed

Kosher salt

POOLISH

2¼ cups (288 g) bread flour

1 cup plus 3 tablespoons (285 g) water, warmed to 105° to 110°F (40° to 43°C)

1 teaspoon active dry yeast

DOUGH

3 cups (384 g) bread flour, plus more for dusting

4 teaspoons sugar

1 teaspoon kosher salt

½ teaspoon active dry yeast

½ cup (120 g) whole milk, warmed to 105° to 110°F (40° to 43°C)

1 egg

4 teaspoons runny honey

TO FINISH

1 egg, for egg wash

2 tablespoons unsalted butter, melted, plus more for greasing

In a medium pot, combine the potatoes with enough water to cover. Salt the water generously, 2 tablespoons of salt per cup of water. Bring to a boil over medium-high heat. Decrease the heat and simmer until the potatoes are fork-tender, about 15 minutes (the time will vary slightly depending on the size of the potatoes). Transfer them to a colander to drain and cool completely. The potatoes need to be completely cooled before being added to the dough; they can be boiled up to 3 days in advance and refrigerated until ready to use.

Mix the poolish. (A poolish is equal weights of flour and water and a small amount of yeast that, when combined prior to making the main dough, boosts flavor and texture in bakes.) In a medium bowl, stir together the flour, water, and yeast until well combined. Cover the bowl with a kitchen towel and set it in a warm, draft-free spot until it is bubbly, about 2 hours.

Make the dough. Pour the poolish into the bowl of a stand mixer fitted with the dough hook. Add the flour, sugar, salt, yeast, milk, egg, and honey and mix on medium-high speed until the dough begins to gather around the hook and pull away from the sides, 4 to 5 minutes. Add the cooked potatoes, squeezing them in your hand as you add them, and mix on low speed until thoroughly dispersed, about 4 minutes. Remove the dough hook and scrape the sides of the bowl, gathering all the dough at the bottom. Cover and let rise in a warm, draft-free place until doubled, about 2 hours.

Butter and line a 9 by 13-inch (23 by 33 cm) baking dish with parchment paper. Place the dough on a lightly floured work surface. Use a bench scraper to portion the dough into eight equal pieces, each weighing about 5.6 ounces / 160 g (use your digital scale for accuracy). Dust the work surface with a bit more flour and then, one by one, shape the portions by flattening each one into an approximately 3 by 5-inch (7.5 by 13 cm) rectangle, with a short side closest to you. Fold the top

CONTINUED

KØBENHAVN
KØBENHAVN

edge (the one farthest away from you) down to meet the middle of the rectangle and then, using just your fingertips, roll the dough into a tight roll and continue to roll it on the tabletop until it measures 5 inches (13 cm) in length. Press on the seam with the heel of your hand to seal. Place it seam side down in the prepared pan, with one end of the bun against one of the short sides of the pan. Repeat with the remaining portions. Place the buns side by side and evenly spaced in two rows, four buns in each row.

Cover and let rise in a warm, draft-free place until the buns are touching each other, about 1½ hours. About 30 minutes before they have finished rising, preheat the oven to 350°F (175°C).

Just before baking, whisk the egg with 1 teaspoon of water to make an egg wash and gently brush the surfaces of the buns. Bake for 30 minutes. Remove from the oven, brush the tops with melted butter, return the dish to the oven, and bake until uniformly browned, 30 minutes more. Once out of the oven, brush with melted butter again. Let cool for 15 minutes in the pan, then gently remove the buns from the pan with a spatula. Break the perforated loaf into individual buns and cut a slit in each if making hot dogs. This bread is best when eaten within a few days and also freezes well together or as individual buns for up to 1 month.

scandinavian-inspired hot dogs

Over the nearly eight years Kantine has been open, we've hosted a slew of Scandinavian hot dog pop-ups in the evening hours, when the restaurant is normally closed. We knew it would be a fun way to introduce the Bay Area to Scandinavian street food, and fun (and sometimes frantic) it has been. Apparently, many of us cannot resist a good hot dog!

When writing each pop-up menu, we aim to find a balance of toppings with traditional flavors and a few modern twists and textures—some soft, others crunchy—and land in the sweet spot of a set of three to four toppings for each kind of hot dog.

A superior dog starts with good bread, and in my opinion, made from scratch is better than store-bought. My bread of choice is a variation on a Danish brioche—Golden Potato Buns (page 226)—but if you want to try something else, try making a hot dog wrapped in flatbread, as they do in Norway with potato flatbread *lomper* (small lefse), or as in Sweden with *tunnbröd,* a soft flatbread spiced with fennel seed, coriander, celery seed, and anise to make a *tunnbrödsrulle.* (You can find both recipes in *Scandinavian from Scratch.*)

Scandinavian hot dogs—the sausage part—come in many sizes, though the most common is longer and thinner than an average American dog. It's totally acceptable that the hot dog pokes out of the ends of the bun or from the top of a hot dog wrap—actually, it's encouraged! Choose a good-quality dog that you prefer. Here in the Bay Area, we love Golden Gate Meat Company's all-beef frank—it's so juicy and has a distinguishing "snap" when you bite into it.

Here are some ideas of what you could put on your dog to create a true Scandi-inspired treat:

tangy + acidic

Pickled Cucumbers (page 47)

Pickled Red Onions (page 48)

Pickled Beets (page 48)

lingonberry sauce (I had this once in Norway—delicious!)

strong Swedish mustard

curry ketchup

creamy + rich

Danish Remoulade (page 60)

mashed potatoes (found in Sweden's *tunnbrödsrulle*)

Horseradish-Dill Cream (page 200)

kebab sauce (popular in norway, similar to garlicky yogurt dressing)

savory + umami

bacon bits

sautéed mushrooms

Swedish shrimp salad (creamy with dill and tiny shrimp, also used in *tunnbrödsrulle*)

crunchy + textured

crispy fried onions (*ristede løg,* a Danish must-have)

crushed potato chips (found in some Norwegian street-style dogs)

shredded romaine lettuce

shredded red cabbage

Malted Sandwich Bread

This bread's subtle sweetness and depth comes from malt powder, which you can find at specialty baking stores or online. Try adding a touch of any leftover malt powder to your favorite waffle or pancake batter for a delightful extra flavor. This recipe can either make one standard loaf or one 8-inch (20 cm) round, perfect for Smörgåstårta (page 167). **MAKES ONE 8½ BY 4½-INCH (21 BY 11 CM) LOAF OR ONE 8-INCH (20 CM) ROUND BREAD**

- 1 cup (240 g) whole or 2% milk, warmed to 105° to 110°F (40° to 43°C)
- 2 teaspoons active dry yeast
- 4 teaspoons malt powder
- 1½ teaspoons kosher salt
- ½ cup (64 g) bread flour
- 2 cups (256 g) all-purpose flour, plus more for dusting
- Neutral oil, for greasing
- 1 egg, for egg wash

Make the dough. In the bowl of a stand mixer, whisk together the milk, yeast, and malt powder by hand. Add the salt and both flours, attach the dough hook, and mix on medium speed until it becomes a homogeneous clump around the hook, about 3 minutes. Transfer the dough to a lightly floured work surface. Knead the dough to thoroughly mix it and develop the gluten until it is a somewhat smooth ball, about 4 minutes. Grease the mixer bowl with oil, plop the dough in the bowl, flip it over to oil its entire surface, and cover with a kitchen towel or plastic wrap. Let the dough rise in a warm, draft-free place until puffy and nearly doubled in size, 1 to 1½ hours, depending on your kitchen temperature.

To shape the dough into a loaf, grease an 8½ by 4½-inch (21 by 11 cm) loaf pan. Turn the dough out of the bowl and onto a lightly floured surface. Use your fingers to gently flatten the dough into a rectangle, where the short side is about 8 inches (20 cm). Form into a loaf by rolling into a tight roll, 8 inches (20 cm) in length. With a bench scraper, transfer the loaf, seam side down, to the prepared pan.

Once again, cover it with a kitchen towel or plastic wrap and let rise until the dough domes just slightly over the edge of the pan, about 1½ hours, depending on the warmth of your kitchen. (It will rise slower in a cool kitchen; don't worry, the additional time will give it even more flavor.)

When the dough is halfway up the sides of the pan, preheat the oven to 425°F (220°C). When the loaf is sufficiently risen, remove the cover, whisk the egg with 1 teaspoon water to make an egg wash, and brush the top of the loaf. Bake for 15 minutes, then decrease the temperature to 350°F (175°C) and bake until golden brown and the internal temperature is 200°F (95°C) when measured with an instant-read thermometer, an additional 20 to 25 minutes. Remove from the oven, let the loaf rest in the pan for 10 minutes, then turn the loaf out onto a rack and let cool completely.

CONTINUED

To shape the dough into a round, grease an 8-inch (20 cm) round cake pan. Turn the dough out of the bowl and onto a lightly floured surface. Use your fingertips to gently flatten the dough into a rudimentary circle. Pull the edges up to the center to create a bit of a ball (though if you said you were seeing more of an oversize dumpling, I couldn't disagree!). Find a new section of your surface where there is less flour and turn your dough ball gathered side down—you should have a nice smooth surface facing up now. Cup your hands around the upper edge of the dough and slide them toward you, moving the dough by only about an inch (2.5 cm). Though it doesn't look like much, this technique creates surface tension on the bread and gives it a gorgeous top crust. Gently lift the ball and rotate it 90 degrees and repeat the same movement with your hands. Continue to pull the dough toward you in this manner a few more times until you have a perky, tight ball of dough. Transfer it to the prepared cake pan. With the heel of your hand, push the dough down to create a disk with about ½-inch (1 cm) gap along the outside edge of the dough.

Once again, cover it with a dish towel or plastic wrap and let rise until the dough's just below the lip of the pan, about 1½ hours, depending on the warmth of your kitchen. (It will rise slower in a cool kitchen; don't worry, the additional time will give it even more flavor.)

When the dough is halfway up the sides of the pan, preheat the oven to 425°F (220°C). When the loaf is sufficiently risen, remove the cover, whisk the egg with 1 teaspoon water to make an egg wash, and brush the top of the loaf. Bake for 10 minutes, then decrease the temperature to 350°F (175°C) and bake until golden brown and the internal temperature is 200°F (95°C) when measured with an instant-read thermometer, additional 15 to 20 minutes. Remove from the oven, let the bread rest in the pan for 10 minutes, then turn the loaf out onto a rack and let it cool completely.

The bread can be stored, wrapped, at room temperature for 4 days or in the freezer for up to 3 months.

Green's Bread

This swirl of soft, tender brioche is a savory spin on the cinnamon knot dough we make at Kantine. I started calling it Green's Bread because of the gorgeous green paste—made with lots of fresh herbs plus a touch of garlic and caraway—that gets smeared over the dough before being shaped. (If you are fond of foraging, try adding or replacing some of the fresh herbs with stinging nettle or nasturtium, see A Forager at Heart, page 239). Baked to a beautiful golden brown, it makes a stunning centerpiece for larger gatherings—a seriously good bread for getting together to pull apart. **MAKES 1 BREAD**

DOUGH

6 tablespoons (84 g) unsalted butter, at room temperature, cut into 1-inch (2.5 cm) chunks, plus more for greasing

1⅓ cups (320 g) whole milk

1 tablespoon instant yeast

1 egg

3 cups plus 2 tablespoons (400 g) all-purpose flour, plus more for dusting

1 teaspoon kosher salt

4½ teaspoons sugar

FILLING

1½ teaspoons caraway seed

1 bunch of flat-leaf parsley

1 bunch of tarragon

1 bunch of chives, thinly sliced

6 tablespoons (84 g) unsalted butter, at room temperature

1 tablespoon extra-virgin olive oil

1 garlic clove, minced

¾ teaspoon kosher salt

TO FINISH

1 egg, for egg wash

Make the dough. Butter a medium bowl and set aside. In the bowl of a stand mixer fitted with the dough hook, combine the milk, yeast, egg, flour, and salt. Mix on low speed until the ingredients are combined, pausing to scrape the sides and bottom of the bowl with a rubber spatula. Increase the speed to medium and mix for 4 minutes more.

Decrease the speed to low and sprinkle in the sugar, 1 teaspoon at a time. Gradually add the butter, one or two chunks at a time, waiting between each addition for them to be incorporated into the dough, then mix for 4 minutes more. The butter should be completely absorbed into a glossy and stretchy dough that is beginning to come off the sides of the bowl.

Transfer the dough to the prepared bowl. Cover it with a kitchen towel or plastic wrap and chill it overnight (up to 12 hours) or let it rest and rise at room temperature for 2 hours, until you are ready to shape it.

Just before shaping the bread, make the filling. In a mortar or spice grinder, grind the caraway seeds. Stem the parsley and tarragon and finely chop their leaves. Together with the chives, you should have about 1½ cups (60 g) herbs total. In a small bowl, stir together the herbs, butter, olive oil, garlic, ground caraway, and salt. Set aside until ready to use. (If you are proofing your dough overnight, I'd suggest making the filling on the second day so that you can avoid having to put the filling in the refrigerator, as it'll be too cold to spread!)

After the dough has rested, it will look puffier and feel slightly drier to the touch. Line a 13 by 18-inch (33 by 46 cm) baking tray with parchment paper. Lightly dust a work surface with flour. Transfer the dough to the prepared work surface and roll it into a 12 by 18-inch (30 by 46 cm) rectangle, situated so that the long (18-inch / 46 cm) end is closest to you, parallel to the edge of your work surface. It doesn't have to be perfectly shaped, but it should come close to those

CONTINUED

dimensions. Try your best to roll it to a uniform thickness and gently pinch and pull at the corners to square them off. If the dough springs back before getting to these dimensions, let it rest for 5 minutes before continuing.

Dollop the filling in small mounds over the dough. Using an offset or rubber spatula, spread the filling over the entire surface of the dough, being sure to cover the edges, too. Starting with a long edge, roll the dough up lengthwise like a jelly roll. Continue rolling the entire piece to even and lengthen it out until it's about 24 inches (60 cm) long. Arrange with the seam side down and, using a chef's knife, cut the roll in half lengthwise. Turn the cut sides to face upward, exposing the stripes of herb filling.

Pinch the two long strands together at one end and begin gently laying the strands one on top of the other, twisting them into a snug spiral while trying to keep the cut sides (with the visible ribbons of filling) facing upward as much as possible. Keep twisting until you reach the end. Then gently coil one end toward the center in a clockwise direction and coil the other end in a counterclockwise direction, to form a figure eight. Tuck the ends under so the bread keeps its shape.

Bring the prepared baking tray as close to your work surface as possible and carefully transfer the bread onto it. Your bread may need a little reshaping once you've placed it on the tray, but don't fuss too much; most irregularities will vanish as the bread proofs and bakes. The bread should measure about 5 by 9 inches (13 by 23 cm) at this point.

Cover the bread with a kitchen towel and set it in a warm, draft-free area until it is noticeably puffier, slightly dry-looking, and the impression of a fingerprint is slow to fill in, about 1 hour for breads that haven't been proofed overnight in the fridge, and about 2 hours for those that have.

When the bread is sufficiently proofed, preheat the oven to 350°F (175°C).

Just before baking, whisk the egg with 1 teaspoon of water to make an egg wash and lightly brush the top of the bread. Bake, rotating the baking tray halfway through, until the bread is puffed and a deep golden brown, 50 to 55 minutes.

Let the bread cool slightly on the tray before transferring it to a rack to cool.

The bread is best enjoyed slightly warm or at room temperature on the day it is baked, but you can store it in an airtight container for 1 day; just pop it in a 350°F (175°C) oven for 10 minutes to reheat.

a forager at heart

I'm by no means an expert forager, but I love the thrill of it. There is something about stepping into nature and discovering edible treasures that allows me to forget everything else and simply focus on the moment. Most of my foraging happens during weekend hikes with my dog, Charlie, either here in San Francisco or somewhere in the seemingly endless green spaces around the Bay Area. The joy only grows when I bring my harvest back home and cook with ingredients I gathered myself.

If you're new at foraging, wild greens are a great place to start your search, as they tend to be found in sizeable quantities and are easy to identify. All the plants below can be found throughout North America and, interestingly, in Scandinavia as well.

forageable greens to look for

Stinging Nettle (*Urtica dioica*): My daughter learned the hard way how to identify this stalky, spike-leaved plant. She also learned that the best way to get revenge on the sting is to cook it and eat it! Nettles are full of nutrients and lose their sting once cooked. Be sure to wear gloves when picking. The young shoots are the most tender. Use them like you'd use spinach: in soups or savory pancakes, or give it a quick blanch and add it to Green's Bread (page 235).

Wood Sorrel (*Oxalis*): A bright, lemony plant known commonly as sour grass. It grows in forests and along trails. The pretty flowers are edible, too.

Lamb's-quarter (*Chenopodium album*): Sometimes called wild spinach, this green is common in urban areas and fields. It's mild, tender, and great for sautéing or adding to omelets.

Nasturtium (*Tropaeolum majus*): An annual crawling plant that I spot often when I'm out for a walk. The entire plant is edible and has a sharp flavor similar to horseradish or mustard. I use it much like I would use arugula, and it is so good in the sauce variation of Roasted String Beans with Basil-Pistachio Sauce (page 106). The bright orange or yellow flowers always brighten a salad, too.

Chickweed (*Stellaria media*): A delicate green that grows year-round in many places; it can often be found stuck to your pant legs after a hike in the wilderness. It has a mild, grassy flavor and makes a great addition to salads or sandwiches.

Dandelion Greens (*Taraxacum officinale*): Dandelion greens are deliciously bitter and lovely in salads or wilted with olive oil and garlic. I harvest them only in early spring, before the plant has flowered, when the greens are sweeter.

Spruce Tips: Spruce tips add a subtle, citrusy resinous brightness that balances a dish. If you're foraging, look for young, soft tips shooting from the trees' higher branches in late spring, around May or June. My favorite species to forage are white spruce (*Picea glauca*) and blue spruce (*Picea pungens*). The tips should be tender and as little bitter as possible; older, tougher tips aren't pleasing to the palate. Try using them in Lamb with Anchovies, Spruce, and Parsley Root (page 213), and even in sweet preparations, too!

Foraging is deeply rewarding but should always be done with care to avoid harvesting anything inedible. I use the PlantSnap app to help with identification after uploading photos of the plants. Never eat anything unless you're absolutely certain of what it is. And always harvest responsibly, taking only what you need and leaving plenty behind for wildlife and regrowth.

Carrot Sheet Pan Bread

This hearty bread is packed with seeds and shredded carrots, giving it great texture and flavor. Unlike a traditional loaf, it's baked as a slab on a baking tray, making it easy to cut into squares. My kids often get frustrated trying to slice a loaf evenly, so this has become their go-to bread—perfect for tearing a corner off, dunking into soup, or splitting open for sandwiches.

MAKES 1 APPROXIMATELY 11 BY 15-INCH (28 BY 38 CM) BREAD

1 tablespoon flaxseed

1 tablespoon sesame seeds

2 tablespoons sunflower seeds

2 tablespoons pumpkin seeds

2 cups (480 g) cold water

1¼ cups (300 g) buttermilk

1 tablespoon active dry yeast

2 to 3 medium carrots, scrubbed and shredded on the large holes of a box grater (about 1½ cups / 155 g)

1⅓ cups (135 g) old-fashioned rolled oats

¾ cup (96 g) whole-wheat flour

1 tablespoon kosher salt

6 cups (768 g) all-purpose flour

2 teaspoons neutral oil, for greasing

Butter, for serving

In a small bowl, combine the flaxseed, sesame seeds, sunflower seeds, and pumpkin seeds. Set aside 2 tablespoons in a separate container for garnishing the top of the bread.

In a large bowl, whisk together the water, buttermilk, and yeast. Add the carrot, oats, whole-wheat flour, and salt and mix well. Add the all-purpose flour and the seed mix (not the garnish) and stir to combine well. (The dough will still be quite wet.) Cover the bowl with a lid or plastic wrap and let it stand at room temperature for 1 hour before refrigerating for a minimum of 6 hours or, preferably, overnight.

When ready to bake the bread, place a baking tray on the oven floor and position a rack in the center of the oven. Preheat the oven to 450°F (230°C). Line a 13 by 18-inch (33 by 46 cm) baking tray with parchment paper, then grease the parchment with the oil.

With the help of a rubber spatula, gently pour the bread dough onto the middle of the tray and, with wet fingertips, carefully press the dough out toward the corners trying to keep as much air in the dough as possible. Aim for a rectangle about 11 by 15 inches (28 by 38 cm). Sprinkle the reserved seeds on top. Immediately put the tray in the oven and throw ½ cup (120 g) water onto the empty baking tray on the bottom of the oven before quickly shutting the door to trap the steam (this helps the bread brown up beautifully).

Bake until lightly golden on top, 45 to 55 minutes. Once baked, slide the bread immediately off the baking tray and onto a rack (don't worry about removing the parchment at this point). While warm, tear into chunks or cut into slices or squares and slather with butter.

This bread is best when eaten within a few days and also freezes well as a whole slab or in smaller chunks for up to 1 month.

Thursday's Savory Oat Pancakes

In Sweden, sweet pancakes are traditionally served *after* Swedish Yellow Pea Soup (page 173), for dessert on Thursdays, but I prefer a savory pancake *alongside* my soup for dunking. This recipe was inspired by Norwegian *grove havrepannekaker,* hearty oat pancakes that are satisfying to eat with soup, or on their own, folded around a filling like smoked trout with crème fraîche and fresh dill or sautéed mushrooms with caramelized onions and a little bit of sharp cheese. And if, by chance, you have leftovers, rolling them up with a bit of jam or butter and cinnamon sugar is never a bad idea.

Be sure to use quick oats so they distribute evenly in each ladleful of batter. **MAKES 10 PANCAKES**

- 1 cup (128 g) all-purpose flour
- ½ cup (50 g) cake flour
- ⅔ cup (70 g) quick oats
- ¼ teaspoon kosher salt
- 4 eggs
- 2 cups (480 g) whole milk
- About 2 tablespoons unsalted butter, for frying

In a medium bowl, whisk together both flours, the oats, and salt until well combined. In a second medium bowl, whisk together the eggs and milk until well combined. Pour half of the liquids into the flour mixture and whisk until well incorporated and no floury lumps remain. Add the remaining liquid and whisk for 1 minute more. Let rest at room temperature for 30 minutes.

Warm a 9-inch (23 cm) skillet or crepe pan over medium heat. Butter the pan. (I usually add about ¼ teaspoon of butter to the pan before cooking each pancake. It's not so much to prevent sticking, but more to promote crispy, lacy edges.) Using a ladle, give the batter a stir, then drop about ⅓ cup (80 g) of the batter onto the pan, lifting and swirling the pan to thinly cover the surface.

Let the pancake cook until the surface looks fairly dry and the edges are browned and lifting slightly away from the pan, 1½ to 2 minutes. Flip it with a spatula and let it cook on the other side for 45 to 60 seconds more. If the pancakes are cooking too quickly, decrease the heat slightly.

Place the pancake on a plate and repeat with the remaining batter, stacking the pancakes as you go. (It's a good idea to keep them warm in a 190°F / 90°C oven while you finish cooking.) Serve immediately.

The pancakes can be stored, covered, in the refrigerator for up to 3 days and in the freezer for up to 1 month.

Flødeboller

(Danish Meringue Puffs)

Okay, three things you need to know before making these: They take time to make, you should read the recipe at least twice before starting, and they are so darn good! At Kantine, our head baker, Hannah, has made them so many times, you'd swear she could do it with her eyes closed. She helped me fine-tune the method here so you can make them successfully at home.

These chocolaty towers resemble oversize Hershey's kisses, but once you bite through the shell and into the fluffy, vanilla-scented meringue, you'll see there's no comparison. In Denmark, these filled treats are sometimes eaten on their own, but just as often they're cracked like an egg on top of an ice cream–filled waffle cone as an extra-sweet treat. Many Danes living abroad miss them dearly—and I got more than a little flack for leaving them out of my first cookbook, so I wasn't about to make the same mistake twice! **MAKES 24 PUFFS**

COOKIE BASE

1 egg (you only need half)

1 cup (128 g) all-purpose flour, plus more for dusting

¼ cup (50 g) sugar

½ teaspoon baking powder

Pinch of salt

2½ tablespoons unsalted butter, at room temperature

1 teaspoon vanilla extract

MERINGUE FILLING

4 ounces (112 g) egg whites (about 3½ egg whites)

¾ cup (150 g) sugar

½ cup (160 g) glucose (available online and at some arts and crafts stores)

½ vanilla bean, slit lengthwise and scraped

⅓ cup (75 g) water

12 ounces (336 g) dark chocolate, chopped (preferably 67% cacao; do not use chocolate chips! See Note, page 247)

2 tablespoons unsweetened shredded coconut (optional)

Make the cookie base. In a small bowl, beat the egg with a fork. Pour half of it (about 1 ounce / 30 g) into a medium bowl and add the flour, sugar, baking powder, salt, butter, and vanilla. Stir the ingredients together, first with a fork, and then once it's a bit shaggy, with your hands. If it seems reluctant to come together, add 2 to 3 drops of water and continue to combine until you have a slightly tacky dough ball. Wrap in plastic wrap and refrigerate for 20 minutes.

Preheat the oven to 350°F (175°C). Line a 13 by 18-inch (33 by 46 cm) baking tray with parchment paper.

Lightly dust a work surface with flour. Using a rolling pin, roll the dough out into a thin, even round about ⅛ inch (3 mm) thick. Using a 2-inch (5 cm) round cookie cutter, cut out as many circles as you can. Transfer the cookies to the prepared baking tray. Press together the dough scraps, then reroll and cut out the remaining rounds. (You should have about 24 cookies. You may have a few cookies left over after piping, but rather too many than not enough!)

Prick each cookie three times with a fork to prevent bubbles. Bake, rotating the tray halfway through, until the edges are light brown, 14 to 16 minutes. Set the tray aside on a rack and let the cookies cool completely while you prepare the meringue filling.

The cookie dough can be made a week in advance and stored in the refrigerator until ready to use. The cookies can be made up to 3 days in advance before topping.

CONTINUED

Flødeboller, CONTINUED

Make the filling. Put a round piping tip (I like Ateco #808 with a ⅝-inch / 1.5 cm opening) into a large piping bag. Make sure that all the ingredients for the meringue filling are measured out before you begin preparing it.

Put the egg whites in the bowl of a stand mixer fitted with the whisk attachment. When you measure out the ¾ cup (150 g) sugar, scoop out 2 teaspoons and set aside. In a small saucepan over medium-high heat, combine the remaining sugar, the glucose, vanilla bean scrapings (save the pod for other uses—there's still lots of flavor in it), and water. Bring the sugar mixture to a boil and cook, using an instant-read thermometer as your guide, until it reaches 242°F (117°C), about 6 minutes. (Refrain from stirring the sugar mixture at any point.) When your sugar gets to 230°F (110°C), start whisking your egg whites on medium-high speed until frothy, then sprinkle in the reserved 2 teaspoons sugar and continue whisking until soft peaks form, while continuing to keep tabs on the temperature of your boiling sugar mixture.

The ideal timing is to have the sugar just reaching the correct temperature at the same time the egg whites have just gotten stiff, so adjust your burner heat and mixer speed if one is happening much faster than the other.

When the sugar is at temperature and the eggs are stiff, decrease the speed of the stand mixer to low and slowly pour in the hot sugar, trying to not pour directly on the whisk, about 1 minute. Turn the speed up to high and continue to beat the meringue until fluffy and the bowl is only just slightly warm to the touch, about 9 minutes.

Immediately transfer the fluff to your prepared piping bag. (If you aren't ready to pipe just yet, transfer the meringue to another bowl so the residual heat doesn't make your meringue flop.) Pipe the meringue onto the cookie bases in 2-inch (5 cm) tall mounds, covering the cookie base from edge to edge with meringue. A damp fingertip can help smooth out any small imperfections afterward.

Let the puffs rest at room temperature for about 2 hours, allowing the fluff to fasten well to the bases and make them easier to dip (head first!) into tempered chocolate.

Dip the puffs. Tempering chocolate is a process of melting chocolate slowly that gives it a smooth and glossy finish and allows it to set well on baked goods. Place three-quarters of the chocolate in a medium heat-resistant bowl. Fill a saucepan with about 1 inch (2.5 cm) of water and bring to a low simmer. Place the bowl over (but not touching) the simmering water. Stir the chocolate occasionally until almost entirely melted.

Remove the bowl from the saucepan (keep the heat on) and stir to melt any remaining bits. Add the rest of the chopped chocolate to the melted chocolate and stir to combine.

Place the bowl back over the simmering water and heat, stirring often, until almost entirely melted. Be sure not to let the chocolate get warmer than 88°F (31°C).

Remove the chocolate from the heat. Dip and roll the puffs into the chocolate, completely coating all sides except the bottom of the cookie base. Let the excess chocolate drip off the tip back into the bowl and then turn and place right side up on a rack to harden. While still wet, sprinkle with the coconut, if desired. If your chocolate gets a little too thick to dip effectively, place it back on the double boiler for a brief moment—remember, no more than 88°F (31°C)—to loosen it up again.

Once the puffs have all been covered, use an offset spatula to turn each puff slightly, so it doesn't end up adhering to the rack. (Save leftover chocolate for future recipes by reheating for 30 seconds in a double boiler to loosen from the sides and scrape into an airtight container.)

Serve the puffs immediately or store in an airtight container at room temperature for up to 3 days.

Note

Chocolate chips contain ingredients that help the chip maintain its characteristic shape, and because of that, the small morsels are rendered unsuitable for tempering. They will simply not result in a crisp, shiny, and streak-free coverage.

Rhubarb Cake
with Custard Sauce

You might think this is absurd, but I miss my rhubarb plants in Copenhagen. There was something about that soil—no matter how many stalks I harvested, the plants would bounce right back with new red shoots. I've cultivated a few plants here in San Francisco, but they don't thrive the same way. They haven't died yet, but I don't dare take a single stalk from them. Thankfully, when it's in season, rhubarb is easy to find at the market, so I can still make this cake and pretend it's from my own plants.

With custard sauce, it's a true dessert, but without it, this makes a lovely snacking cake that can be eaten for *fika* (see page 250), even while on a picnic or hike. **MAKES ONE 9-INCH (23 CM) CAKE**

CUSTARD SAUCE

- 1 cup (240 g) whole milk
- ½ cup (120 g) heavy cream
- 1 vanilla bean
- 5 egg yolks
- ¼ cup (50 g) sugar
- Pinch of kosher salt

CAKE

- About 1 pound (454 g) rhubarb, ends trimmed
- 1¼ cups (160 g) all-purpose flour
- 2 teaspoons baking powder
- ½ teaspoon baking soda
- ½ teaspoon kosher salt
- ½ cup (113 g) unsalted butter, at room temperature, plus more for greasing
- 1 cup (200 g) plus 2 tablespoons sugar
- 2 eggs
- 2 teaspoons vanilla extract
- ⅓ cup (85 g) crème fraîche or sour cream

Make the custard sauce. In a small saucepan over medium-low heat, warm the milk and cream until steaming. Using a paring knife, split the vanilla bean lengthwise and use the back of the knife to scrape out the seeds. Add the pod and seeds to the warm milk mixture. Remove from the heat, cover, and set aside to steep for 15 minutes.

In a medium bowl, whisk together the egg yolks, sugar, and salt until pale yellow. Whisking constantly, slowly pour the warm milk mixture into the yolk mixture. Return the mixture to the saucepan and place over medium-low heat. Warm the sauce gently, stirring constantly, until it thickens enough to coat the back of a spoon, about 4 minutes; do not let the mixture boil or cook too rapidly or the eggs will scramble. Pour the custard sauce through a fine-mesh sieve into a jar or airtight container. Let cool, then refrigerate until ready to use.

Make the cake. Preheat the oven to 350°F (175°C). Grease a 9-inch (23 cm) round springform pan with butter, then dust with flour.

Unless the rhubarb stalks are very thin, split the stalks lengthwise into ½-inch (1 cm) wide pieces. Trim the pieces into lengths that can be placed parallel to one another in the pan, so the longest stalks are in the middle and decrease in size toward the two sides. Set aside. Chop any leftover rhubarb into ¼-inch (6 mm) pieces and set aside; you should have about ½ cup (60 g).

In a small bowl, whisk together the flour, baking powder, baking soda, and salt. In a medium bowl, using an electric mixer, beat together the butter and 1 cup of the sugar on medium-high speed until light and fluffy. Add the eggs, one at a time, beating well after each addition. Add the vanilla extract and beat on low speed until combined. Scrape

CONTINUED

down the sides of the bowl. Add half the flour mixture and beat on low speed just until combined, then stir in the crème fraîche. Add the remaining flour mixture and the reserved rhubarb trimmings and beat just until combined.

Scrape the batter into the prepared pan and smooth the top. Gently lay the reserved long pieces of rhubarb on top without pushing them into the batter. Sprinkle evenly with the remaining 2 tablespoons sugar.

Bake until the cake is golden brown and a toothpick inserted into the center comes out clean, 45 minutes. Transfer the cake pan to a rack and let cool in the pan for about 10 minutes. Run a knife around the sides of the cake to loosen it, release the sides of the pan, and slide the cake directly onto the rack. Let cool completely.

To serve, pour some of the custard sauce onto a plate and top with a wedge of cake.

fika

Scandinavians cherish their coffee breaks, not always for the sake of the coffee, but often for the conversations as well as the baked goods that are enjoyed alongside. In Sweden, these breaks are known as *fika*. Similar rituals exist in Denmark and Norway as well, but in my opinion, the Swedes are the true masters of the tradition. In workplaces, fika typically happens twice a day, first around 10 a.m. for *förmiddagsfika* (the morning break) and again around 3 p.m. for *eftermiddagsfika* (the afternoon break). But fika isn't limited to office life—it's just as common to meet a friend for a casual catch-up over coffee and something sweet. If this sounds like a ritual you could get behind, you might enjoy my first book, *Scandinavian from Scratch,* where you'll find plenty of recipes perfect for fika.

Almond Waffles

with Apple Marmalade and Caramelized Almonds

These almond waffles are crisp on the outside, tender on the inside, and it's surprising how much the nuttiness of the almond flour comes alive as they cook. Topped with sticky, caramelized-apple marmalade and crunchy almonds, they're meant for breakfast or brunch but could just as easily be served for dessert—especially with a scoop of ice cream, a dollop of lightly whipped cream, or even a spoonful of skyr for a tangy contrast.

The apple marmalade and caramelized almonds can be made ahead, making it easy to pull everything together when it's time to eat. MAKES 12 WAFFLES

APPLE MARMALADE

4 tart-sweet baking apples (1½ pounds / 680 g), such as Pink Lady or Fiji

½ cup (100 g) packed light brown sugar

½ cup (100 g) granulated sugar

2 tablespoons fresh lemon juice

2 tablespoons unsalted butter

CARAMELIZED TOASTED ALMONDS

1 tablespoon unsalted butter

1 cup (110 g) sliced almonds

¼ cup (50 g) granulated sugar

Pinch of kosher salt

ALMOND WAFFLES

4 eggs

½ cup (100 g) granulated sugar

1½ cups (192 g) all-purpose flour

½ cup (52 g) almond flour

½ teaspoon baking soda

½ teaspoon kosher salt

2 cups (480 g) buttermilk

7 tablespoons (100 g) unsalted butter, melted, plus more for greasing

Ice cream, whipped cream, or skyr, for serving (optional)

Make the apple marmalade. Core the apples, leaving the peel on, then slice lengthwise into thin slices, about ⅛ inch (3 mm) thick. Add to a large bowl, then add both sugars and the lemon juice. Toss to coat evenly, then set aside for 15 minutes to macerate.

In a large skillet over medium-high heat, melt the butter. Add the apples, leaving any juice in the bowl for later. Cook, stirring occasionally, until the apples release their juices, the juices evaporate, and the apples begin to caramelize and soften, about 10 minutes. Add the reserved juices in the bowl to the apple mixture and stir to combine. Continue to cook until the apples become sticky, 2 to 3 minutes longer. Transfer to a bowl. (The marmalade can be made in advance and stored in an airtight container in the refrigerator for up to 1 week.)

Make the caramelized almonds. Line a baking tray with parchment paper or a silicone mat. Wipe out the skillet you used for the apples and place it over medium-high heat. Melt the butter, then add the almonds, sugar, and salt. Cook, stirring constantly with a wooden spoon, until the sugar melts and the almonds are toasted and fragrant, about 4 minutes; decrease the heat to medium-low during the last minute or so of cooking to ensure the almonds don't burn. Immediately transfer the almond mixture to the prepared baking tray and spread into an even layer using the spoon. Let cool completely, then crumble into pieces.

Make the waffles. Preheat the oven to 190°F (90°C) and place a tray in the oven. Preheat a waffle iron, preferably heart-shaped, on high heat for 15 minutes while you prepare the batter.

In a medium bowl using an electric mixer fitted with the whisk attachment, beat together the eggs and sugar on medium-high speed

CONTINUED

until the mixture thickens and turns pale yellow, about 3 minutes. In another medium bowl, whisk together the flour, almond flour, baking soda, and salt. Add the flour mixture to the egg mixture and beat on low speed to combine, then stir in the buttermilk and melted butter. Do not overmix.

Brush the waffle iron with butter before cooking the first waffle (you probably won't need to grease it after that). Add ½ cup (115 g) of the batter onto the hot waffle iron and close the lid. Cook until the waffle is golden brown, 3 to 6 minutes, or according to the manufacturer's instructions; adjust the heat as needed so the waffle cooks evenly. Transfer the waffle to the baking tray in the oven to keep warm and repeat to make all the waffles with the remaining batter.

To serve, top each waffle with some of the apple marmalade and the caramelized almonds, as well as a dollop of ice cream, whipped cream, or skyr, if you like.

Saffron-Poached Peaches

with Yogurt Panna Cotta

Since I already wrote a baking book, I wanted to keep the number of baking recipes in this non-baking book to a minimum. Sometimes, having those kinds of restraints leads to more creativity than you'd expect—this recipe is proof of that.

I've long adored saffron, not just for its floral flavor and striking color but for the magical quality it seems to have. Here, two flavors that go very well together, saffron and peaches, are united. Choose freestone peaches that are flavorful and ripe but still slightly firm. If saffron isn't your thing, swap it out for a split vanilla bean instead, seeds and pod included. MAKES 6 SERVINGS

YOGURT PANNA COTTA

- 2 tablespoons water
- 1½ teaspoons unflavored gelatin powder
- 1 cup (235 g) heavy cream
- 6 tablespoons (85 g) sugar
- 2 cups (500 g) plain whole milk yogurt (not Greek yogurt)
- 1 tablespoon vanilla extract

POACHED PEACHES

- 2½ cups (590 g) water
- 1 cup (200 g) sugar
- 3 ripe but slightly firm peaches (about 1¼ pounds / 550 g), halved
- Peel of 1 orange, removed in strips with a vegetable peeler
- ½ teaspoon saffron, lightly crushed

Make the panna cotta. Place the water in a small bowl, then sprinkle the gelatin over the water. Let stand until the gelatin softens, about 10 minutes. Lightly spray six ¾-cup ramekins or custard cups with cooking spray or, alternatively, grease lightly with neutral oil.

In a medium saucepan over medium-high heat, combine the cream and sugar, stirring constantly until the sugar dissolves. Bring the mixture just to a low boil, stirring occasionally, then remove the pan from the heat and stir in the gelatin mixture until it dissolves. Transfer to a large glass measuring cup and let the mixture cool to lukewarm, stirring often.

Stir the yogurt and vanilla into the cream mixture. Divide the mixture evenly among the prepared ramekins. Transfer the ramekins to a baking tray and cover with plastic wrap, making sure it doesn't touch the tops of the panna cotta. Refrigerate until set, about 4 hours or up to 2 days.

Make the poached peaches. In a straight-sided medium saucepan, combine the water and sugar and bring to a boil over high heat. Decrease the heat to medium and place the peaches gently in, cut side down, together with the orange peel and saffron. Cover with a lid. Adjust the heat so that the liquid simmers gently and poach the peaches until just tender and not mushy, 7 to 12 minutes depending on the ripeness of the fruit. Remove from the heat. Let the peaches and poaching liquid cool completely to room temperature. Fish out and discard the orange peel from the poaching liquid. Gently remove the skins of the peaches and discard. If serving the same day, let the peaches remain at room temperature. If preparing a day or two in advance, transfer the peaches in their cooking liquid to an airtight container and store in the refrigerator for up to 2 days.

To serve, run a small sharp knife around the panna cotta in each ramekin. Set a plate atop each ramekin and invert, allowing the panna cotta to settle onto the plate. Place a peach half on top of each panna cotta and serve chilled, drizzled with a little of the golden-flecked poaching liquid.

Raspberry "Silk" with Dark Chocolate

Every time I make this dessert, I am taken back to my early days in Denmark. It's not a traditional Danish dessert, but it was so simple and satisfying that my friends and I would whip up a batch nearly every time we ate together. It quickly became our go-to sweet—so much so that we eventually decided to go cold turkey. Slowly, we forgot all about it.

It wasn't until recently that I remembered our "sweet habit" and tried to re-create the recipe. By then, everyone had forgotten their memorized versions, but when I served it on my last trip to Denmark, it was like reuniting with an old friend. My friends and I started reminiscing, not just about the dessert but about all the other little moments that we shared around that time.

Aside from chopping the chocolate, there's almost no prep, and the whole thing comes together in under 10 minutes. Its perfectly pink color always turns heads, but what makes it truly special is the tartness of the raspberries. I've tried making it with other berries, but nothing quite matches their bright, tangy contrast against the richness of the heavy cream and dark chocolate.

MAKES 4 TO 6 SERVINGS

10 ounces (280 g) frozen raspberries

3 tablespoons sugar

1½ cups (360 g) heavy cream

2 ounces (56 g) bittersweet chocolate (minimum 70% cacao), chopped, plus more for garnish

In a blender or food processor, combine the raspberries, sugar, and cream. Pulse, stopping often to scrape down the sides, until well blended, then add the chocolate and pulse to combine. Pour into small glasses or bowls, garnish with a bit more chocolate, and serve immediately.

Red Fruit Soup

In Danish, this dessert is called *rødgrød med fløde,* literally "red porridge with cream," though in this type of porridge, there are no grains—just peak-season berries (and sometimes rhubarb) gently simmered into a silky and tart fruit soup.

Fruit porridges are common across Scandinavia, from blueberry to rose hip, made with fruit harvested at the height of its season. A piece of advice about sugar: Start with less—you can always serve a little extra at the table for those who want more sweetness.

If you ever visit Denmark, be prepared: Danes delight in hearing foreigners trip over the famously tricky name of this dessert in Danish. It took me ages to master it myself, but now it rolls off my tongue as smooth as the cream that gets poured over each serving. **MAKES 4 SERVINGS**

2 pounds (900 g) any combination of washed and hulled raspberries, strawberries, or red currants

4 ounces (112 g) rhubarb (cut in bite-size pieces), blueberries, or black currants

1 vanilla bean

Pinch of kosher salt

1 cup (240 g) water

½ cup (100 g) sugar, plus more as needed and for serving

2 tablespoons cornstarch

Up to 2 tablespoons fresh lemon juice

½ cup (120 g) ice-cold heavy cream (or whole milk, if preferred), for serving

½ cup (50 g) toasted sliced almonds (see Toasting Nuts and Seeds, page 42)

Place the berries and rhubarb in a medium heavy-bottomed pot. Split the vanilla bean lengthwise and, using a paring knife, use the back of the knife to scrape out the seeds. Add the pod and seeds, the salt, and water to the pot. Bring to a quick boil, then skim off and discard any impurities on the surface. Decrease the heat to medium-low, cover, and simmer, stirring occasionally, until the berries have broken down to a mush, 8 to 10 minutes. Remove the pot from the heat and discard the vanilla bean.

Some people (like my mother-in law) prefer their fruit porridges to be smooth. In that case, use an immersion blender to liquefy the fruit chunks at this point.

Stir in ¼ cup (50 g) of the sugar, give it a taste, and add more, if needed. (The amount needed depends on individual taste and the berries' natural sweetness.)

In a small bowl, stir together the cornstarch and 2 tablespoons of cold water and whisk it into the hot fruit porridge. The consistency should be slightly thickened, just enough to coat the back of a spoon. Transfer the porridge to a heat-resistant container, sprinkle a little bit of sugar on top to prevent a skin from forming, and let it cool to room temperature. The porridge can be served at room temperature or chilled. If you prefer it cold, place it in the refrigerator for at least 3 hours but preferably overnight. Before it's served, I like to add a touch of lemon juice, if the porridge needs an extra zing.

Ladle the soup into four shallow bowls and serve with a small bowl of sugar, a small pitcher of cream, and the almonds. (Some people always add more sugar, while others prefer a little pucker in their fruit porridge.)

The porridge can be made in advance and stored in a lidded container in the refrigerator for 5 days.

Rum Balls

As a bakery café owner, I can vouch for the fact that leftover pastries are a thing. In Scandinavia, bakeries have long found clever ways to repurpose day-old danishes, brioche, and cake scraps, and one of the best ways is to make rum balls, *romkugler*. At home, I stockpile leftover baked goods—a half muffin here, a heel of a banana bread there—in a bag in the freezer until I have enough to make a batch.

The elements of a good rum ball are below, but they can be made to your liking: Red berry jam adds fruitiness, but other jams work just as well. The rum extract can be omitted if you prefer. Not a fan of coconut? Roll them in cocoa powder or finely chopped almonds instead. However you finish them, they're an easy, no-bake treat worth making. **MAKES 16 BALLS**

1 pound (454 g) leftover pastry, muffin, and/or cake scraps

3 tablespoons almond paste (not marzipan)

3 tablespoons red berry jam

¼ cup (27 g) cocoa powder

1 teaspoon vanilla extract

1 teaspoon rum extract

Pinch of kosher salt

¼ cup (20 g) unsweetened shredded coconut

Cut the leftover pastry scraps into bite-size pieces and place in a food processor. Chop until uniform in size. Add the almond paste, jam, cocoa powder, vanilla, rum extract, and salt and process until the mixture comes together into a thick dough. (If yours isn't quite coming together, add a few drops of water.)

Remove the dough from the bowl and roll into a long log about 16 inches (40 cm) in length. (If your dough seems a bit too sticky, refrigerate it for about 20 minutes to make it easier to work with.) Cut the log in half (use a ruler if you want to be extra precise), then each half in half again, and then each quarter into four pieces.

Put the coconut into a shallow bowl. Roll each piece into a ball and roll into the shredded coconut to coat, if desired.

The rum balls can be stored in an airtight container in the refrigerator for up to 2 weeks.

acknowledgments

This second book has conjured memories I hadn't revisited in years and allowed me to retrace my path. I could never have imagined that my first trip to Denmark in the summer of 1990 would be so transformative—or that meeting Malene Eikers, the Danish exchange student who had attended my high school in Ohio years earlier, would change the course of my life. Malene, "Mor" Else, and Anne, thank you for fully opening your hearts, home, and family to me. I will be forever grateful.

To the entire staff at Ten Speed Press—so many talented individuals have helped nurture and enrich this book, including my dedicated editor, Cristina Garces, and associate art director Lizzie Allen. Many thanks to my agent, Katherine Cowles, who has been my steady and supportive guide every step of the way. And to Aaron Wehner, it has been an extraordinary privilege. Thank you for your kindness and trust.

To my recipe testers and developers Leith Brooks Barry, Kim Laidlaw, Jennie and Ben Smith, and my daughter Rosa Majholm—thank you for your meticulousness and perseverance in making each and every recipe work well.

Jennifer Aaronson, thank you for your giddiness, honesty, and wholehearted investment. Picking up where we left off after *Scandinavian from Scratch* has been a dream. You bring talent, insight, and inexplicable enthusiasm to every adventure. Thank you for styling this book, traveling beside me, and being a very dear friend. More to come!

For the stunning images in these pages, I am filled with gratitude to have had the fortune of having worked with San Francisco–based Molly DeCoudreaux and Copenhagen-based Mikkel Vang. Thank you for your expertise, ideas, and patience. It was a complete joy to be in creative "bubbles" with you both.

Kantine, my fourth child, thank you for the past eight years. Our local community (and their insistence on getting the recipe for the savory porridge!) inspired this book. It wouldn't have been possible without the dedicated team that keeps things running smoothly, despite my book deadlines: Dedan Hyatt, Hannah Jacobson, Max Harnden-Castillo, Leydi Cauich, and the rest of the team, thank you.

To the farmers, vendors, and purveyors who provide us with beautiful, inspiring ingredients: Cheers to you for making it easier for us to create delicious, meaningful food.

Leaving Denmark ten years ago was one of the hardest and most rewarding things I've done. Though my family and I still feel the distance, it's all the more special when loved ones there welcome us back each visit with warmth and good food, making us feel like we never left. Thank you to the families of Rachel Curtis Gravesen, Christine Aghassipour, Paula Holm, Line Schou, Caroline Gjerulff, Martin Michael Hansen, Daniel and Rebecca Majholm, Fredrik Hillerbrand, Thit Folke Lehmann, and Lone Voss.

To my sister, Kim Shin, and my brother, Matt Accettola: Together we have been able to keep the memory of our mom and her love of food and family alive.

To my life partner, Joachim Majholm, thank you for making me smile, standing by my side, and growing with me. Together with our three kiddos—Rosa, Calvin, and Louis—there's never a dull moment!

And finally, thank you to my dear dog, Charlie, who follows me everywhere and is always ready to cuddle.

Index

D

E

F

N

O

P

Q

R

S

Ten Speed Press
An imprint of the Crown Publishing Group
A division of Penguin Random House LLC
1745 Broadway
New York, NY 10019
tenspeed.com
penguinrandomhouse.com

Typefaces: Rasmus Andersson's Inter and Klim Type's Tiempos

Library of Congress Cataloging-in-Publication Data has been applied for.

Hardcover ISBN 978-0-593-83778-8
Ebook ISBN 978-0-593-83779-5

Editor: Cristina Garces | Production editor: Terry Deal
Designer: Lizzie Allen
Production designers: Mari Gill and Faith Hague
Production: Serena Sigona
Prepress color managers: Nick Patton and Zoe Tokushige
Food and prop stylist: Jennifer Aaronson
Prop assistant: Madge McCulloch
Props furnished by Cosita, Rosendahl Design Group US, and Fritz Hansen
Copy editor: Heather Rodino | Proofreaders: Miriam Taveras, Rachel Whitten, Lydia O'Brien | Indexer: Barbara Mortenson
Publicist: Jina Stanfill | Marketer: Andrea Portanova

Manufactured in China

10 9 8 7 6 5 4 3 2 1

First Edition

The authorized representative in the EU for product safety and compliance is Penguin Random House Ireland, Morrison Chambers, 32 Nassau Street, Dublin D02 YH68, Ireland, https://eu-contact.penguin.ie.